A 'CONNOISSEUR'S PANORAMA'

Thomas Girtin, *Study for the 'Eidometropolis' Section Four: The Thames from Westminster to Somerset House* (detail); see Fig. 6.

A 'CONNOISSEUR'S PANORAMA'

Thomas Girtin's *Eidometropolis*
and Other London Views, *c.* 1796–1802

by
Greg Smith

Edited by
Sheila O'Connell

LONDON TOPOGRAPHICAL SOCIETY
Publication No. 180
2018

©

LONDON TOPOGRAPHICAL SOCIETY
312 Russell Court
London, WC1H 0NG
2018

ISBN
978 0 902087 67 5

PRODUCED IN GREAT BRITAIN BY
SCORPION CREATIVE

CONTENTS

AUTHOR'S ACKNOWLEDGEMENTS

My primary debt is to my wonderful editor, Sheila O'Connell, who commissioned the book and steered it through every stage of its writing and production with great skill and good sense, taking great pains, in particular, with the images. Together with the designers, Graham Maney and Steve Hartley, she showed enormous strength of mind to pause the production of the book whilst pursuing an image of the newly discovered drawing for section five. Graham also displayed a commendable flexibility, finding a way to incorporate such important new material at the very last possible moment. For help with pro-curing the image from Roderick Zinsser, and thanks to him of course, I would like to mention my colleagues at the Yale Center for British Art at New Haven, particularly Cecie Clement, Matthew Hargraves and Scott Wilcox.

Scott, a great authority on the panorama, is just one of a number of fellow curators and art historians who have generously shared their expertise, answered my questions or read the text in one form or other. I would like to single out Gabriele Koller who generously passed on her discovery of a possible new fate for the *Eidometropolis* in Eastern Europe in the 1820s. Many thanks also go to Tony Gee who advised on the history of prizefighting in this period. Amongst colleagues who read the text for us can I mention Hugo Chapman and Kim Sloan from the British Museum, and thank Anne Lyles and Ian Warrell as well. The research for the book required a wide range of visits to libraries and museums and I would like to single out particularly the staff of the Print Room at the British Museum for their enthusiastic support. Thanks too to the staff of the Paul Mellon Centre for Studies in British Art for providing me with research facilities and support.

And, finally, can I add special thanks to my wife, Liz Hall, for all her support and also acknowledge the help of Karin Southorn with the translations of foreign reviews.

CREDITS

INTRODUCTION

It is exactly fifty years since Hubert Pragnell published *The London Panoramas of Robert Barker and Thomas Girtin* for the London Topographical Society, and in revisiting part of the same territory in 2018 some justification is in order.[1] The intervening period has seen the discovery of three preparatory drawings by Thomas Girtin (1775–1802) for the *Eidometropolis*, the name he coined for his London panorama of 1801–02. Moreover, the rapid expansion of online searchable texts in the last decade has thrown up a wealth of new material which has considerably enhanced our understanding of Girtin's monumental lost work. My own starting point in what has become a very rewarding re-engagement with Girtin's 360-degree view of London from near Blackfriars Bridge was the discovery of an extraordinary document in The National Archives, uncovered by a random internet search in 2010.[2] A hitherto unrecorded law case in the Court of Chancery in London in 1804 saw Thomas Girtin's widow, Mary Ann, sue his brother John for the income generated after the artist's death by the *Eidometropolis* and sales of his works. The unsuspected wealth of detail about the production and consumption of the panorama found in the claim and counter-claim documents prepared by the two protagonists more than justify a new study on their own. The unique character of online searches is that they turn up results in areas where researchers would either not think to look or dismiss as not worth the effort. Discoveries in this category, including a newspaper announcement of the sale of the panorama which pre-dates its previously accepted completion date and two unknown descriptions of the panorama hiding under a misspelling of the artist's name, have expanded the documentary material revealed by the law case. Significant studies of panoramas in general have also been published, but, whilst these have often employed sophisticated theoretical tools, they are not always factually well grounded. The new research aids that have become available to the students of topographical views can, I suggest, provide a better foundation for such surveys, as well as

adding detail to the necessarily sketchy older accounts.

That process has already begun in the case of the other part of Pragnell's pioneering study, the London panorama from the Albion Mills of Robert and Henry Aston Barker.[3] Together with Peter Jackson, Ralph Hyde showed in his 1988 London Topographical Society publication how the prints produced by Henry Aston Barker and Frederick Birnie (1792–93) as a souvenir of the earlier London panorama (Figs 12–14) contain a wealth of accurate topographical information. It is my contention that the outlines and coloured drawings that Girtin produced as preparatory works for each of the seven sections of the 360-degree panorama, eleven of which survive (Figs 1–11), may be analysed in the same way. With the key that Hyde and Jackson produced and a copy of Richard Horwood's near contemporary map of London to hand (Fig. 36),[4] they too can be shown to display a substantial level of detail and positional accuracy. Girtin's drawings may have been produced in preparation for a 'connoisseur's panorama', with complex light and weather effects, but at the heart of the project was a solid core of topographical fact, and this is worth re-examining if we are to appreciate the unique character of his approach.

The other aspect of the digital information revolution that justifies a new study of the *Eidometropolis* is the sheer quantity of visual material that has become accessible to researchers. The digitization of the topographical collections of the British Museum, the London Metropolitan Archives (Collage), the Museum of London and the British Library, to name just the most important, have revealed a mass of images of the city, many unknown even to specialists. The beautiful drawings Girtin made in preparation for his panorama are rightly celebrated, but we now have evidence of an army of artists, professional and amateur, whose efforts to record every facet of the city illustrate equally what was revolutionary about Girtin's London view and what had already been well documented by his contemporaries and predecessors.

Fig. 1   Thomas Girtin, *Study for the 'Eidometropolis' Section One: The Albion Mills*,
c. 1801, pencil and pen and brown ink, squared for transfer on wove paper, 28.8 × 53 cm,
British Museum, London (1991,1109.16).

Fig. 2   Thomas Girtin, *Study for the 'Eidometropolis' Section One: The Albion Mills, c.* 1801, pencil and watercolour on laid paper, 32.8 × 54.1 cm, British Museum, London (1855,0214.24).

Fig. 3   Thomas Girtin, *Study for the 'Eidometropolis' Section Two: Great Surrey Street and Christ Church, Southwark*, *c*. 1801, pencil, pen and brush and brown ink, squared for transfer on wove paper, 28.1 × 50.5 cm, Yale Center for British Art, New Haven (B1977.14.4325). A manuscript note in pen and ink by a previous owner on the back of the drawing is visible in the centre of the sheet.

Fig. 4   Thomas Girtin, *Study for the 'Eidometropolis' Section Three: Lambeth and Westminster*, *c*. 1801, pencil and pen and ink, squared for transfer on wove paper, 32.5 × 53.8 cm, British Museum, London (1991,1109.15).

Fig. 5   Thomas Girtin, *Study for the 'Eidometropolis' Section Three: Lambeth and Westminster*, *c*. 1801, pencil and watercolour on laid paper, 29.2 × 52.5 cm, British Museum, London (1855,0214.23).

Fig. 6   Thomas Girtin, *Study for the 'Eidometropolis' Section Four: The Thames from Westminster to Somerset House*, *c.* 1801, pencil and watercolour on laid paper, 24 × 53.8 cm, British Museum, London (1855,0214.27).

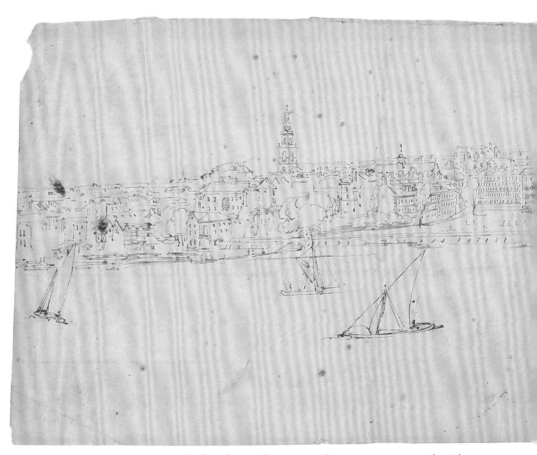

Fig. 7   Thomas Girtin, *Study for the 'Eidometropolis' Section Five: The Thames from the Temple to Blackfriars, c.* 1801, pencil and pen and and ink on wove paper, 16.2 × 44.8 cm, collection of Roderick D. Zinsser, Jr.

Fig. 8   Thomas Girtin, *Study for the 'Eidometropolis' Section Five: The Thames from the Temple to Blackfriars*, *c.* 1801, pencil and watercolour on laid paper, 21.1 × 48.4 cm, British Museum, London (1855,0214.25).

Fig. 9   Thomas Girtin, *Study for the 'Eidometropolis' Section Six: Blackfriars Bridge and St Paul's Cathedral*, *c.* 1801, pencil, pen and ink and watercolour, squared for transfer on wove paper, 35.2 × 51 cm, British Museum, London (1855,0214.26).

Fig. 10   Thomas Girtin, *Study for the 'Eidometropolis' Section Seven: Blackfriars Bridge to Albion Mills*, *c*. 1801, pencil and pen and ink, squared for transfer on wove paper, 23.6 × 50 cm, London Metropolitan Archives (q8972599).

Fig. 11   Thomas Girtin, *Study for the 'Eidometropolis' Section Seven: The Thames from Queenhithe to London Bridge*, *c.* 1801, pencil and watercolour on laid paper, 20.7 × 44.5 cm, British Museum, London (1855,0214.28).

CHAPTER ONE

The Thames from the Adelphi, *c*.1796

The *Eidometropolis* was not Girtin's first essay in the panoramic mode, but the character and significance of the remarkable 180-degree view that the young artist drew from a window in the Adelphi Terrace overlooking the Thames a few years earlier is difficult to appreciate fully. Despite every effort, the three extended drawings remain untraced, having last been seen in 1912, and the images shown here are reproduced from black and white photographs taken then (Figs 12–14).[5] There is, however, enough detail to confirm the attribution to Girtin and to give an approximate date of 1796 to the extended scenes, equivalent to three double-page spreads, which, connected together, form a panoramic view of the river looking south.[6] The three views were almost certainly made from one of the upper windows of the residence of Dr Thomas Monro, at whose Adelphi home, no. 8 to the west end of the Royal Terrace, Girtin and his exact contemporary J. M. W. Turner worked during the winter months of 1794–98.[7] It is very likely that Monro comm- issioned the drawings as a record of the spectacular river view that he inherited when he moved into the luxury development of the Adam brothers in the spring of 1794. The view the drawings depict fits with the location of Monro's residence and the title matches an item sold at his posthumous sale in 1833, 'the Thames from the Adelphi'.[8]

The fact that the drawings remained in the patron's possession is crucial to an understanding of their essentially private function, very different from the public spectacle of the 360-degree *Eidometropolis*. An elevated window in the Adelphi may have opened up a view of a vast circuit, but there is a fundamental difference between the panoramic, however extensive, and the true panorama. A view from a window could never form the basis of a 360-degree presentation, but the similarity between the format of these drawings and the outlines that Girtin produced as a preparation for his later public project have

persuaded some to wrongly assume that they were a first thought for a monumental panorama. The carefully defined outlines and a close attention to architectural detail, which might allow us to identify many of the buildings depicted, encouraged a misreading of their function. Moreover, Girtin uses a similar format for both the drawings from the Adelphi and the studies for the *Eidometropolis*, dividing the extensive view into smaller units; in the former, the extensive lateral view is broadly equal in proportion to two of Girtin's standard landscape compositions. The crucial difference, however, is that the Adelphi drawings do not contain a grid, essential for scaling up an outline to a larger-scale canvas, and this, together with the viewpoint adopted, confirms their status as a private commission.

The other context in which these drawings have been discussed is the panoramic views east and west along the river from Somerset House that, following the influential example of Giovanni Antonio Canal (Canaletto), formed a staple part of the repertoire of many British landscape artists from the middle of the eighteenth century.[9] Given that Girtin's drawing style was based on Canaletto's to a degree, it is not surprising that writers on the artist have drawn attention to the similarity in the com- position between Girtin's view from Somerset House to the Shot Tower (Fig. 12) and Canaletto's drawing of the *View from Somerset House Gardens Looking Towards London Bridge*, which was engraved by Edward Rooker (Fig. 15).[10] Equally, the new generation followed the same template, with St Paul's rising above the forest of City spires and towers as the river bends to the right and the Surrey bank links visually with the northern shore. There are, however, two crucial differences between Girtin's drawings and the extended prospect east and west from this point of the river which suggest that the similarities with Canaletto are coincidental at best. The first

Fig. 12 Thomas Girtin, *A Panorama of the Thames from the Adelphi Terrace, Section One: Somerset House to Blackfriars Bridge, c.* 1796, pencil, pen and brush and ink on paper, *c.* 15.2 × 45.7 cm (from a photograph taken *c.* 1911).

Fig. 13 Thomas Girtin, *A Panorama of the Thames from the Adelphi Terrace, Section Two: The Surrey Bank, c.* 1796, pencil, pen and brush and ink on paper, *c.* 15.2 × 45.7 cm (from a photograph taken *c.* 1911).

Fig. 14 Thomas Girtin, *A Panorama of the Thames from the Adelphi Terrace, Section Three: Westminster Bridge to York Stairs, c.* 1796, pencil, pen and brush and ink on paper, *c.* 15.2 × 45.7 cm (from a photograph taken *c.* 1911).

Fig. 15 Edward Rooker, after Antonio Canaletto, *A West View of London with the Bridge, Taken from Somerset Gardens,* 1750, etching and engraving, 26.1 × 40.2 cm, British Museum, London (1880,1113.1432).

is that the elevated viewpoint adopted by Girtin, which turns the foreground into a complex pattern of riverine shapes, omits the polite interactions and sociable context of earlier views and pushes the commercial life of the city into the distance. The second difference only comes into focus when we turn to the third section of Girtin's panoramic drawing (Fig. 14), covering the riverside just west of Westminster Bridge, the bridge itself and the abrupt termination of the view in a building to the west of the Adelphi. Canaletto and his British followers also produced a similar view to create a panoramic pair to the view east from Somerset House gardens, and the composition from that position was balanced and satisfying. Two extended views, attributed to both Paul and Thomas Sandby, *View to the West from the Gardens of Somerset House* (Fig. 16) and *View to*

Fig. 16 Paul Sandby, attributed to, *View from the Gardens of Somerset House, Looking West,* c. 1770, pencil, watercolour and pen and ink on paper, 48.3 × 195.1 cm, British Museum, London (G,13.30).

Fig. 17 James Peller Malcolm, *The River Thames at York Stairs*, 1797, watercolour on paper, 28.6 × 42.1 cm, British Museum, London (1880,1113.1373).

the East from the Gardens of Somerset House, provide a good example of the way that, in the former, the buildings to the right, including the Water Tower at York Buildings (Fig. 17), act as a *repoussoir* and the bend of the river leads into a fine prospect of Westminster Bridge.[11] In comparison, this mighty symbol of engineering excellence and a source of civic pride assumes a rather prosaic appearance from Girtin's more

elevated position and the great national monuments of Westminster Abbey and Westminster Hall back into, or are submerged, by their humble surroundings. Whilst Paul (or Thomas) Sandby was free to choose the position that produced the most satisfactory composition, Girtin's commission fixed him to a location which, although it worked well in one direction, resulted in an unsatisfactory disorder in the other.

Arbitrary and unfocused outcomes such as these, where topographical significance is compromised, are a key characteristic of the panorama, constituting the most significant link between the earlier private commission and the public spectacle of the *Eidometropolis*.

Turning to the middle section of the panoramic study from the Adelphi (Fig. 13), we can begin to appreciate another challenge posed by the adoption of a wide-angle view; namely, how to preserve pictorial unity across different types of scenery. In the Canaletto model adopted by Paul or Thomas Sandby, the paired views, with their matching bends of the river and cultivated gardens in the foreground, leave little room for the Surrey bank. In Girtin's view, in contrast, the south bank with its cluttered mix of timber yards, boatyards, iron foundries, breweries and a myriad of manufacturers, including the Coade Stone Works, make up exactly half of the drawings' extent. Thomas Monro's view from his windows at the Adelphi may have encompassed a perfect Canaletto composition to the east, but the vista south was more problematical in pictorial terms and Girtin responded by adopting a different set of landscape conventions. Beginning with the Albion Mills at the south-east end of Blackfriars Bridge, Girtin highlights a few landmarks such as, from left to right, the square tower of St Saviour, Southwark, the monumental form of Watt's Patent Shot Tower and then Christ Church, Southwark, each of which we will see again. But the detail then gives way to a looser style of draughtsmanship in which a more extensive use of wash captures the textures of building materials on the banks and the predominantly rural character of the scene behind. It is possible to make out the large Assembly Room of Cuper's Gardens, abandoned as the focus of the old pleasure gardens and now occupied by a vinegar manufacturer, but the rest is a picturesque jumble in which the industrial merges into the rural. The effect recalls any number of Dutch landscapes, but particularly Rembrandt's etching, *View of Amsterdam from the North-West* (*c.* 1641), which extends to form just such a panoramic scene with a mix of the rural and the industrial compressed into a narrow belt in the middle ground.[12] Girtin's extended view is still essentially an outline drawing and unsuited to the depiction of the sort of light and atmospheric effects which unify the *Eidometropolis*, and, arguably, he did not have at his command in 1796 the formal means to employ weather effects or industrial smoke to unify the

different components of a fractured composition. The smoke from Lukin's Iron Foundry that dominates section three of the *Eidometropolis* (Fig. 5) is absent here, and, tellingly, the factory itself cannot be identified.

The challenge that Girtin faced in conceptualizing the Surrey bank can be better appreciated when we consider the novelty of his task. Though there is a surprisingly rich iconography of views of the south bank, none are both so extensive and brought as close as Girtin's. Instead, artists took up a position on the bank and, as in numerous examples by Daniel Turner (*fl.* 1782–1810), use a building on the shore to direct the eye along the riverside to either Blackfriars Bridge with St Paul's behind (Fig. 18) or Westminster Bridge with Westminster Abbey beyond. The formula worked if, as here, the distant point of interest was not overshadowed by the foreground. In this case the monumental form of the Shot Tower is invested with a timeless quality without labouring figures or overt signs of industry. Other generalized views of timber yards, boatyards and wharves feature in the foregrounds of views of both of the great eighteenth-century bridges, but only very occasionally, as in John William Edy's print, *A View from King's Arms Stairs, Narrow Wall, Lambeth Marsh* (1791), are the scenes anything more than generic.[13]

There was, however, one other extended view of the south bank seen from the north, an etching dated 1807 and titled *Southwark, from an Elevated Situation at the Back of the Beaufort Buildings, Strand* (Fig. 19). The anonymous print is poorly executed and this rare impression is not in good condition, but as an unusual early-nineteenth-century elevated view of the south bank between Blackfriars and Westminster bridges it deserves our attention. This is even more the case because of the inscription on the verso, which records that it was made 'From a drawing by Malton', presumably referring to Thomas Malton the younger whose posthumous sale in 1804 contained 'Sketches for a Panorama of London'.[14] Girtin copied a number of Malton's prints, producing watercolour versions of his London views for John Henderson, a neighbour of Thomas Monro's at no. 4 Adelphi Terrace, and if the drawing for this print was by Malton there is a possibility that Girtin knew of it. Indeed, it was Malton who suggested that the view from Blackfriars Bridge is so 'extensive and various' that only the 'newly invented Panorama' could do

Fig. 18   Thomas Sutherland and Daniel Turner, after Daniel Turner, *View of Blackfriars Bridge and St Paul's*, 1803, hand-coloured aquatint, 33 × 44.9 cm, Yale Center for British Art, New Haven (B1977.14.15380).

Fig. 19   Anonymous, *Southwark, from an Elevated Situation at the Back of the Beaufort Buildings, The Strand*, 1807, etching, from two plates, 44.4 × 111.8 cm, British Museum, London (1880,1113.1205).

it justice.[15] A word of caution, though. By adding smoke from various sources and dividing the landscape into broad areas of light and shade, the anonymous etcher might have been inspired in his depiction of a mix of manufactories and wharves with a rural hinterland by the example of Girtin's *Eidometropolis*. On balance, though, it would seem that Malton, or whoever was responsible for the original drawing, found a more credible way of conveying the magnitude of modern London and the particular character of the south bank than Girtin's deployment of picturesque Dutch landscape conventions in his views from the Adelphi.

There are two other drawings of the Thames at Blackfriars Bridge that have erroneously been associated with Girtin's panoramic view from the north and the panorama from the south bank. The fact that both images were taken from a low viewpoint alerts us again to an all too common misunderstanding of the distinction between the panorama proper and the panoramic mode. A drawing in the Morgan Library, New York, hitherto titled *The Thames: Blackfriars Bridge and St Paul's Cathedral from the Adelphi* (Fig. 20), is the more impressive work and initially, at least, suggests that Girtin tried out an alternative lower view to the Monro sheets.[16] However, the location has been misidentified, as the view was actually taken from further upriver, and this is confirmed by the discovery of a strikingly similar

scene in etching and aquatint after an amateur artist, Margaretta Elizabeth, Baroness Arden, which is inscribed 'from the House of M. A. Taylor Esqr Whitehall'.[17] The profusion of architectural detail might again suggest a connection with Girtin's earlier panoramic drawing, but another print after the work has recently emerged, an engraving simply titled *London* by John Greig (1804), and this opens up intriguing new possibilities (Fig. 21).[18] This second print, which exactly follows the Girtin drawing at the Morgan Library, rather than the panoramic format of the slightly earlier aquatint, is nonetheless inscribed 'from a Drawing by the R[t]. Hon.[ble] Lady Arden'. The superior quality of the draughtsmanship means that we can discount the possibility that it is simply misattributed to Girtin, and the most likely scenario is that he was employed by a publisher to work up the amateur's drawing into something more polished. Girtin therefore took Lady Arden's drawing (whereabouts unknown), as his point of departure and converted the panoramic composition into a

Fig. 20   Thomas Girtin, *The Thames with St Paul's and Blackfriars Bridge*, pencil on paper, 13 × 18.4 cm, Pierpont Morgan Library, New York (1994.8).

traditional landscape format by including more sky and a lively framing device of shipping in the foreground, adding a Thames barge lowering its mast to the right. The fact that it is Baroness Arden's name that accompanies the print is indicative of the audience the publication was aimed at, and also offers a reminder of the significant role of non-professionals in documenting the image of London. Indeed, Arden's view should be seen in the context of a series of panoramic sketches made by Girtin's most famous pupil, Amelia Long, Lady Farnborough (Fig. 22). Again using the Shot Tower as a *repoussoir* to lead the eye to the bridge and St Paul's, Long's rapidly applied watercolour washes recall her master's coloured drawings for the *Eidometropolis*, even if they, too, are viewed from a low position and are similarly panoramic.[19]

Another panoramic London vista, *The North Bank of the Thames with St Bride's, St Paul's and Blackfriars Bridge* (Fig. 23), has been linked to Girtin's *Eidomtetropolis*, presumably on the basis of the subject, a view from the south bank, and, more particularly, because of the inscription: 'For a Scene'.[20] Moreover, the drawing includes a grid, suggesting that it was made to be enlarged. Girtin supplied designs for theatrical sets and, since the low viewpoint alone means that it could not have been produced in relation to a 360-degree panorama, it is much more likely that the 'Scene' was a stage set.[21] Whether the drawing is by Girtin is another question. The rather mechanical treatment of the architectural features of the buildings bears some resemblance to the Arden drawing (Fig. 21) and, indeed, to passages of the outlines made for the *Eidometropolis* (Fig. 10),

Fig. 21   John Greig, after Margaretta Elizabeth, Baroness Arden (Thomas Girtin), *London*, 1804, engraving, 13.2 × 19 cm, Yale Center for British Art, New Haven (B1977.14.18474).

Fig. 22   Amelia Long, later Lady Farnborough, *St Paul's and Blackfriars Bridge*, *c.* 1800, pencil and watercolour on paper, 16.2 × 41 cm, Yale Center for British Art, New Haven (B1986.29.441).

Fig. 23   Thomas Girtin, attributed to, *The North Bank of the Thames with St Bride's, St Paul's and Blackfriars Bridge*, *c.* 1798, pencil, watercolour and pen and ink, squared for transfer on laid paper, 15.6 × 43.8 cm, London Metropolitan Archives (q8972665).

but the quality of the draughtsmanship is arguably not sufficiently high to attribute it confidently to Girtin. From the end of the 1790s, many panoramic views were painted for theatrical productions, commissioned by impresarios who wished to take advantage of the success of the Barkers' innovatory public spectacle.[22] The drawing was therefore probably produced by one of the numerous but poorly documented painters who worked in the theatre.

Misunderstanding the function of drawings such as these, as well as the Monro sheets themselves, is more forgivable when the work they are said to relate to has long since been lost.

Moving from Girtin's panoramic view from the Adelphi to the lost panorama itself other challenges arise. Girtin's preparatory drawings certainly help us to understand aspects of the appearance of the *Eidometropolis*, but there are limits, and so the discoveries of new documentation, which open up fresh ways of comprehending Girtin's contribution to the spectacular depiction of London topography, are particularly welcome. Before turning to examine the subject of the *Eidometropolis*, therefore, we need to outline the details and implications of those new discoveries.

CHAPTER TWO

The *Eidometropolis*: new evidence for understanding its production, promotion and consumption

Thomas Girtin proudly announced in the first advertisement for his new project on 2 August 1802 that

> his GREAT PICTURE of LONDON 108 feet long, and 18 feet high, taken from the top of the British Plate Glass Warehouse near Blackfriars-bridge [...] will, if Mr. Girtin's health permits, be open for exhibition THIS DAY [...] at Mr. Wigley's Great Room, Spring-Gardens.[23]

The mention of the artist's poor health which resulted in his premature death later in the year has led a number of writers to suggest that Girtin must have begun work on his canvas well before this opening date, with one authority arguing that it was begun as early as 1797.[24] Two pieces of new evidence provide a clearer picture of the project's genesis and confirmation that it was substantially complete a year ahead of its opening. The first is an advertisement from the *Morning Chronicle* of 14 October 1801 which announced

> TO be SOLD by PRIVATE CONTRACT, a large PICTURE, intended to form an Exhibition upon the Plan of the Panorama, representing an extensive VIEW of LONDON [...] by Mr. Thos. Girtin'.[25]

The notice continues that it is

> presumed, from the general effect and manner in which the subject is treated, that it is an object of importance, and that it might be exhibited to considerable advantage on the Continent.

Interested parties are directed to 'Messrs. Greenwood and Co. at their Auction Room, Whitcombstreet, Leicester-square'. The second piece of new evidence is even more specific. John Girtin records that he made the following payments in the autumn of 1801 on behalf of his brother to 'his men employed in painting the picture of London':

> 7 September, £2
> 8 September, £5
> 19 September, £12 2s.
> 26 September, £9 19s. 6d.
> 4 November, 10s. 6d.
> 9 November, £4 4s.[26]

From these sources it is possible to plot the changing plans that Thomas, and latterly his brother John, had for what subsequently was called the *Eidometropolis*. Thus, although there is no evidence of when Girtin made his preparatory drawings, work on painting the monumental canvas was clearly underway by the summer of 1801. The artist seems to have had little idea of the costs involved in producing a panorama on such a scale, however, and as early as September he was unable to pay the men he employed on the project and turned to his brother for financial help. Offering the canvas for sale suggests that whatever plans Girtin might have had at the outset for how and where the panorama was to be displayed circumstances had changed.[27] Certainly, the date of the advertisement for the sale of the 'VIEW OF LONDON' in October 1801 indicates a significant change in thinking which was presumably precipitated by the artist's realization that on his own he lacked the capital to carry the project through. The recent signing of the preliminaries of the Peace of Amiens opened up a new opportunity for the canvas to be shown abroad, something that would not have been possible when it was begun when almost all contact with the Continent was blocked. The advertisement in the *Morning Chronicle* did not result in a sale, however: John Girtin recorded a few weeks later that Thomas, 'being unable to leave London for want of money', applied to him for assistance, and that John agreed to 'lend and advance the sum of a hundred pounds and four shillings [...] towards defraying the expenses of the Journey' to Paris.[28] Thomas left the country on 20 November, presumably carrying with him the monumental canvas.

The next twist is recorded in a newly discovered notice in the *Morning Post* from the beginning of February 1802, stating that 'GURTIN has been denied the privilege of exhibiting his *Panorama* in Paris, comprehending a view of London, taken from the British Plate Glass Manufactory'.[29] The problem, no doubt, was that Girtin's plans were thwarted by the enforcement of the French patent for panoramas by its owner, the entrepreneur James Thayer.[30] Girtin returned to London in April 1802 and it was at this point that he resurrected the plan to show the work here, and, having run through his brother's substantial loan of the previous year, it was agreed, according to John Girtin, that he became a full partner in the project. Thomas thus agreed that John should 'exhibit the said Picture in London [...] on the account of the said Thomas Girtin and that he [...] should receive the admission money for such Exhibition and should defray all the charges and expenses'.[31] By the time the panorama finally opened in August 1802, its projected audience had changed on three occasions, therefore, begging the question of whether Girtin sought to tailor it to the different expectations and interests of viewers first in London, then in Paris, and finally, and successfully, in London.

Estimates of how long the painting of the *Eidometropolis* took have hitherto been based on the assumption that Girtin executed the work himself. This assumption was encouraged by contemporary accounts of the project, which stressed Girtin's personal involvement. Edward Edwards, for instance, specifically claimed that Girtin's panorama 'was painted by himself'.[32] In fact, it was always likely that Girtin received help with painting such a large canvas, and the same advertisement that offered the panorama for sale in 1801 also stated explicitly that the 'large PICTURE' was 'taken [...] from Drawings painted by Mr. Thos. Girtin'.[33] Later advertisements, however, announced it as 'GIRTIN'S GREAT PANORAMA', with variations on that assertion of authorship, suggesting that the artist was aware that he had naively given the game away in his first pronouncement, and subsequently his name was made central to the show's marketing. At this distance it is not possible to say exactly how much work was undertaken by assistants, but, since it is likely that the payments made by John were only part of the total laid out to others, it appears that a substantial part of the production, at least as it stood in November 1801, was delegated by Girtin. It may even be possible to identify one of the 'men employed in painting the picture of London'. John records an unpaid sum of £9 3s. 8d. to a

Mr Andrews, who may have been Robert Andrews (*fl.* 1789–1818), a scene painter who worked at Sadler's Wells where a number of Girtin's views were adapted as scenery.[34]

The involvement of others in the production of the '1944 square feet' of canvas employed in the panorama means that, whatever the visual delights of the outlines and coloured drawings Girtin prepared for each of the seven sections of the 360-degree view, we must remember that they were primarily made for the use of others to work from. In the case of the outlines (Figs 1, 3, 4, 7, 9, 10), this entailed transferring the grid to the canvas stretched on a circular armature and then copying the very detailed drawing, taking care to adapt the perspective so that the straight lines drawn by Girtin would not subsequently appear curved to the viewer at the centre of the circle. The involvement of assistants in this process might indeed have been inferred from a note scribbled by Girtin on the outline for the final section, which reads 'leave out this vesel', referring to the sailing barge in the foreground (Fig. 10). For the assistant working from the coloured drawings (Figs 2, 5, 6, 8, 11) the operation was less mechanical. Here one can imagine that the task was to block out on the canvas the main areas of colour and establish the broad effects of light and shade and the textures and tones of the different constituent parts of the scene. Girtin had had very little experience with oil paint at this date, having produced just one work, shown at the 1801 Royal Academy exhibition, and so, whilst it is easy to see why he needed practical help, it is not so simple to establish what his own involvement entailed. There are two related issues which, when we know that Girtin was not responsible for all of the production process, might help to establish this point. Firstly, there is the notion that in a collaborative process what is absent or lacking from the drawings might indicate what the artist planned to add to the canvas himself. And, secondly, differences between what the textual sources tell us about the panorama's appearance and the two sets of drawings might also provide clues about where the involvement of assistants ended.

Perhaps the most intriguing omission from Girtin's drawings is that, whilst they cover the whole 360 degrees in seven sections, none of them extend to the panorama's full height, and, as can be seen in the extended strips (Fig. 30), variations in the height of the colour drawings in particular indicate substantial missing areas. The advertisements the Girtin brothers ran for the *Eidometropolis* stress its large size — '108 feet long, and 18 feet high', 1,944 square feet (about 180 square metres) — in which case the seven drawings that make up the circle should each fill a grid of 18 by roughly 15½, and each measure the same size. Some of the drawings have been trimmed at the edges in later years to tidy them up and make them more saleable, but others, such as for sections five (Fig. 8) and seven (Fig. 11), never showed more than a narrow strip. It is possible that the Girtins exaggerated a little; thus, whilst the canvas may have been 18 feet high, the viewing platform obscured areas at the top and bottom. However, the main reason why the coloured drawings, in particular, are missing whole areas is because Girtin presumably left areas of the river, the sky and the foregrounds to be improvised by himself on the canvas. Close to the spectator, the latter would have been particularly challenging for an assistant to render to a satisfactory illusive standard, and it is here that Girtin no doubt made his most significant contribution to the canvas.

The relatively small part of the river that is shown in the coloured drawings for sections four, five and seven (Figs 6, 8 and 11) may have been partly due to the view being obscured by the roof of Albion Place Terrace and the need here to invent the missing areas. However, the instruction to his assistant to omit the sailing barge prominently featured in the foreground of section

seven also suggests why the river required Girtin's particular attention. Thus, compared to the Barkers' panorama from the Albion Mills (Figs 24–25) and, indeed, any number of London views which stressed the important role played by the Thames in images of the city, whether as a source of trading wealth, a place of leisure or the site of royal and civic pageantry, Girtin's coloured drawings feature relatively few boats. That this was true for the *Eidometropolis* as well is suggested by the souvenir etching produced by F. L. T. Francia (Fig. 26), which does not include any sailing barges at the Albion Mills Wharf, as well as by a review of its Paris showing. The writer accused the painter, assumed to be French, of having 'let his patriotic feelings get the better of him', since the ships around the Tower of London 'are all but invisible'; continuing that 'Along the Thames near [...] *Blackfriar's Bridge* one sees only three or four miserable little fishing boats, although [...] this stretch of the famous river is crowded with vessels of every kind'.[35] The most perceptive of the British reviewers, in the *Monthly Magazine*, understood that the role played by the Thames in a panorama by a landscape artist famed for his subtle natural effects was more sophisticated than a simple signifier of wealth or imperial might. 'The water is pellucid, and, contrary to what we have generally seen in pictures of this description', he wrote, it 'varies in its colour; that near the shore very properly partaking of the hue of the earth

Fig. 24   Henry Aston Barker and Frederick Birnie, *Panorama of London from the Roof of Albion Mills. Plate Two: Albion Place*, 1792, etching and aquatint, 42.8 × 52.1 cm, British Museum, London (1880,1113.1200).

Fig. 25   Henry Aston Barker and Frederick Birnie, *Panorama of London from the Roof of Albion Mills. Plate Three: Blackfriars Bridge*, 1792, etching and aquatint, 42.8 × 52.1 cm, British Museum, London (1880,1113.1200).

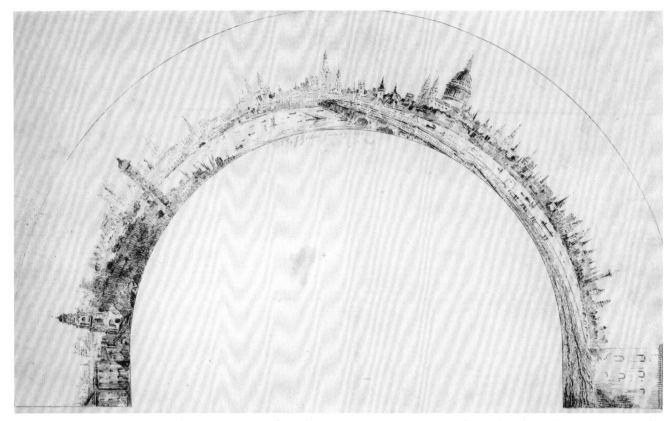

Fig. 26 François Louis Thomas Francia, after Thomas Girtin, *Panorama of London from Westminster to the Tower, after Girtin's 'Eidometropolis'*, 1803, etching, 22 × 37 cm, British Museum, London (1863,0110.98).

beneath', whilst the craft upon the river are 'boldly and forcibly relieved'.[36] In other words, the river and its craft partake of a landscape aesthetic of subtle and naturalistic effects which might appeal to 'the connoisseur'. This can be seen at its best in section four (Fig. 6) where, although it is possible to discern the characteristic form of a Thames sailing barge with its flat bottom and a mast which might be lowered, as well as a wherry, used as a water taxi, the forms are generalized and the artist's primary interest lies in the patterns the vessels and their wakes make in the water. Calm water invariably features in the foregrounds of Girtin's watercolours, producing broad reflections and patterns of flat colour, and it is to be expected that he would take up the task of reproducing such a characteristic part of his signature style on the canvas, omitting in the process a vessel too close to the viewer to depict in such a generalized manner.

Only three of the seven sections feature figures, and they are confined to a bold diagonal that links Blackfriars Bridge, Albion Place and Great Surrey Street (sections six, one and two, Figs 9, 1 and 3). Two of the coloured drawings for these sections have not been traced, but there is

evidence that they existed, in which case they may have followed the format of the preparatory drawing for section one (Fig. 2) where the figures are left as uncoloured outlines, again suggesting that this was Girtin's province and not something for his assistants to work on.[37] This assumption is supported by textual evidence because, although the figures are quite difficult to read, even in the outline (Fig. 1), they do not look as though they are engaged in anything so unsavoury as the 'ring surrounding two pugilists' in 'Blackfriars-road' noted by one reviewer.[38] This detail was assumed to be a case of the reviewer confusing Girtin's panorama with the Barkers' which, according to the key published to accompany its Paris showing in 1802, included a scene of pugilism (Fig. 28). However, the recent discovery of a notice which describes a boxing scene as an integral part of Girtin's *Eidometropolis* raises fascinating questions, not least which of the two depictions of a ring came first. '*Belcher* and *Burke*, we suppose, are the two combatants in Mr. GIRTON'S *Eidometropolis*', the writer begins, noting that the scene 'must afford great pleasure to the amateurs of pugilism, as well as of painting'. The 'ring is well drawn',

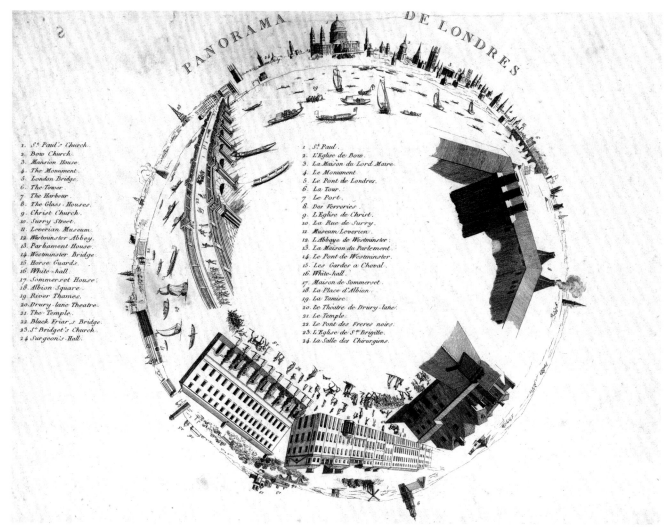

1. St. Paul's Church.
2. Bow Church.
3. Mansion House.
4. The Monument.
5. London Bridge.
6. The Tower.
7. The Harbour.
8. The Glass-Houses.
9. Christ Church.
10. Surry Street.
11. Leverian Museum.
12. Westminster Abbey.
13. Parliament House.
14. Westminster Bridge.
15. Horse Guards.
16. White-hall.
17. Sommerset House.
18. Albion Square.
19. River Thames.
20. Drury-lane Theatre.
21. The Temple.
22. Black Friar's Bridge.
23. St. Bridget's Church.
24. Surgeon's-Hall.

1. St. Paul.
2. L'Eglise de Bow.
3. La Maison du Lord Maire.
4. Le Monument.
5. Le Pont de Londres.
6. La Tour.
7. Le Port.
8. Des Verreries.
9. L'Eglise de Christ.
10. La Rue de Surry.
11. Museum Leverien.
12. L'Abbaye de Westminster.
13. La Maison du Parlement.
14. Le Pont de Westminster.
15. Les Gardes a Cheval.
16. White-hall.
17. Maison de Sommerset.
18. La Place d'Albion.
19. La Tamise.
20. Le Theatre de Drury-lane.
21. Le Temple.
22. Le Pont des Freres noirs.
23. L'Eglise de St. Brigille.
24. La Salle des Chirurgiens.

Fig. 27   Anonymous, after Henry Aston Barker, *Panorama de Londres: A Key to the Barkers' Panorama of London from the Roof of Albion Mills*, c. 1802, etching and engraving, 30.6 × 40.7 cm, British Museum, London (1880,1113.5509.2).

Fig. 28   Detail of Fig. 27.

the review continues, 'and the variety of characters flocking to the battle, are truly humoursome'.[39] In fact, there is no way that Girtin depicted James or Jem Belcher, the champion pugilist and his dogged challenger, the 'bruising butcher' Joseph Bourke. Their very

public and acrimonious rivalry featured two fearful beatings for Bourke and other aborted meetings as police and magistrates intervened to prevent public disorder; certainly, there was no fight in the environs of Blackfriars Bridge.[40] Their first bout in November 1801 also occurred whilst

Girtin was in France and the second took place after the panorama's opening in August 1802. Given the public interest in the combatants, any depiction of pugilists at this date might have been interpreted as referring to the two men, and Girtin presumably included a set of combatants because the subject was topical. But at what point did he substitute them for the figures shown in Figures 1 and 2? It is unlikely that he would do so for a French audience, and the changes were probably introduced after his return to London in April 1802 when he looked to add a contemporary note to his year-old canvas.

From an art-historical perspective, the introduction of pugilists into what was otherwise celebrated as a scene of subtle landscape effects tailored to the 'connoisseur' comes as a surprise. The description of 'the variety of characters flocking to the battle' as 'truly humoursome' suggests that Girtin strayed into the territory of genre painting, or the more light-hearted drolleries of Thomas Rowlandson. But this is to forget the setting of the action, the shell of the Albion Mills which, for all of its outward classical sobriety, was a deserted ruin, allegedly the result of the ire of an enraged mob. This was a marginal site, boarded up to keep out the humblest traders who eked out a living in Albion Place just like the figure of *A Poor Sweep, Sir!*, one of the *Cries of London*, by William Marshall Craig, that frequents a contemporary image of this end of Blackfriars Bridge.[41] Southwark, south of the river and the site from Shakespeare's time of a lower sort of entertainment, demanded a suitable subject from Girtin and a change of plan saw the introduction of something harder edged.

The low subject matter depicted here was not something the Girtin brothers emphasized in the wide range of advertisements and notices they paid to insert in the daily and weekly press on what was an unprecedented scale for a panorama.[42] Promoting a new panorama of London carried a particular challenge which they initially struggled with: namely, how to convey to the public the nature of the spectacle in a way which distinguished it from previous shows. The earliest advertisements indicate that they were loath to use the word panorama itself, choosing instead to announce Girtin's 'GREAT PICTURE OF LONDON'.[43] By 25 August, however, Thomas admitted that since 'it has been conceived to be merely a Picture framed', he directed 'the Public to notice that it is Panoramic, and from its magnitude, which contains 1944 square feet, gives

every object the appearance of being the size of nature', and the emphasis on the work's size was thereafter a constant in its promotion.[44] The challenge of making the spectacle sound like something that had already caught the public's attention at the same time as reassuring the audience that Girtin's panorama was new, was surely the impetus behind the introduction in mid-August of a new title, the *Eidometropolis*.[45] As with the word panorama, this was a learned neologism, coined from Greek, meaning the 'image of the capital', and it was designed to signify novelty within an established convention that flattered the visitor's erudition. From this point the terms became fixed, the spectacle was the 'EIDOMETROPOLIS; or, GIRTIN's GREAT PANORAMA of LONDON'.[46]

The difficulty with this strategy was that, as earlier visitors to the Barkers' panorama of London from the Albion Mills knew, the Girtins were offering very little in terms of content that was different. The set of six prints made after the Barkers' first panorama displayed between 1791 and 1794 show that from Girtin's viewpoint on the other side of Albion Place the same range of buildings are visible, with St Paul's and Blackfriars Bridge dominant, and great landmarks such as Westminster Abbey and the Tower of London distant and partially obscured (Figs 24–25). The only significant addition which stemmed from the projects' different viewpoints is that Albion Place Terrace features prominently in the foreground of the Barkers' view (Fig. 24), whilst the Albion Mills, the site of their viewing position, dominate Girtin's view in the opposite direction (Fig. 2). As Ralph Hyde has pointed out, Albion Place was the best position from which to create a panorama of London with a fine view of St Paul's and the bend of the river providing a twin focus, east and west, of the City and the West End, together with a broad expanse of water in the foreground.[47] In 1795–96, when the Barkers produced a second larger panorama of London (covering 2,700 square feet) for the Upper Circle of their specially constructed building in Leicester Square, they chose the same view again. With no obvious alternative, therefore, the Girtins needed to establish that their panorama was different, and it was this that presumably led them to consistently misrepresent the viewpoint that the artist had used, claiming that it was 'taken from the top of the British Plate Glass Manufactory near Blackfriars-bridge'.[48] This was doubly incorrect. In the first instance, the manufactory was actually in St Helens, Lancashire and, as the print shows (Fig. 29), it was the warehouse that looked over the Thames at Blackfriars Bridge. The same image, and Figure 24, also show how Girtin could not have worked from the warehouse roof as the taller Albion Place Terrace would have blocked his view. Unlikely as it seems, Girtin must have perched on the roof of the terrace to make his drawings (Fig. 3). For customers in search of novelty as well as spectacle, Albion Mills and Albion Place Terrace sounded too alike.

Girtin's *Eidometropolis* may have featured only a handful of sites not shown by the Barkers, but this was still a view of London, and the Girtins unsurprisingly announced that the 'situation is chosen, as to show to the best point of view' of the city's most famous and historically significant sites.[49] Another notice proudly proclaimed that

> the subject will be found interesting from the beauty of the Thames, with Somerset-house, Temple Gardens and a variety of other objects that adorn its banks; the grandeur of Westminster Abbey, St. Pauls, and combinations of other Churches, &c. in the City, too numerous to mention; the elegance of Blackfriars Bridge, the Monument, the Tower, the Surrey Hills, &c. &c.[50]

The primacy of the subject, the city and its most prominent monuments, was at the heart of the promotion of the spectacle, as it was with the other London panoramas of the day. The Girtin brothers followed existing precedents in another respect, emphasizing that the spectacle was truly deceptive, immersive and real, and it was they who were presumably responsible for passing on a telling anecdote to *Bell's Weekly Messenger*. The recently deceased king's composer, Samuel Arnold, 'was so fascinated with Mr. GIRTIN's Eidometropolis', it claimed, that he 'lay himself all along on the platform viewing this matchless production of art for two hours and upwards, expressing the greatest satisfaction, as do all that see it'.[51] And following Thomas's death in November, John Girtin repeatedly highlighted the 'deceptive power' of his brother's work, emphasizing the 'astonishing correctness of perspective' employed.[52] This, he claimed, 'is allowed by all the most eminent in the Profession, to surpass anything of the kind ever yet seen.[53]

What is striking about the advertisements in general is that none of them stress the unique selling point of Girtin's *Eidometropolis* as identified both in the reviews and by the artist's obituarists. Here, they stated, is a 'connoisseur's

Fig. 29 Anonymous, *The British Plate Glass Warehouse*, 1790, hand-coloured etching and aquatint, 10.4 × 18.3 cm, British Museum, London (G,8.91).

panorama' in which artistic values of 'harmony' and truth to nature produce a 'most picturesque display', with one anonymous author claiming that the work fills the 'mind with the most copious and perfect idea of the sublime'.[54] This 'exquisite production of art' was the work of an 'artist' who 'trusted to his eye', rather than a mere mechanic who took 'the common way of measuring and reducing the objects' in the view.[55] Girtin introduced into his 360-degree view of London a range of light and weather effects controlled by an overarching pictorial harmony that critics appreciated as the work of an 'uncommon artist'.[56] The advertisements, in contrast, merely emphasize that the view also includes 'the surrounding Country to the most remote distance', something that was well within the capabilities of the average scene painter.[57] The question therefore is whether the Girtins missed a trick in not emphasizing what was different about the *Eidometropolis*, rather than trying to establish that the spectacle was 'gratifying to the common observer'.[58]

Here we are helped by the recent discovery of the attendance figures for the panorama's first five months which show that, despite the assertion of the *Monthly Magazine* that 'Mr. Girtin's Eidometropolis [...] is very well attended', the numbers were far from healthy.[59] John Girtin's accounts thus reveal that the income from the sale of tickets equalled £101 7s., amounting to 2,020 visitors at a weekly average of only ninety-two.[60] The best week only saw 159 admissions, and this had trailed off to seventy-five at the time of Thomas's death; moreover, the subsequent publication of complimentary accounts of the panorama failed to significantly increase the numbers. This was slim pickings compared to attendances at the Barkers' panoramas, with one estimate giving a figure of 40,000 a year for just one of their presentations in the specially constructed building.[61] To be blunt, the *Eidometropolis* was a commercial failure, and this was undoubtedly a consequence of the project's uncertain and contradictory inception. The Barkers' second London panorama closed in 1796 and they moved on to display a range of more exotic locations and topical subjects. Girtin was surely right to think that his smaller panorama, taken from virtually the same location, was more suited to a foreign audience unfamiliar with the scene and its various presentations. The London public by 1802 was clearly sated with views of their city from near Blackfriars Bridge, and this

was compounded by the Girtins' decision to concentrate the publicity for their spectacle on its topographical subject matter. A lack of novelty put off the popular audience and the number of 'connoisseurs' attracted by the artful treatment of the subject was ultimately insufficient to cover the costs of the enterprise.

The degree to which the *Eidometropolis* covered well-trodden ground has, in fact, been hitherto underestimated. Online searches of newspapers and periodicals have thrown up a mass of advertisements and notices for another large-scale panorama of London that toured Scotland and the English provinces between 1798 and 1803, with a final showing in Dublin.[62] The 'GRAND PERSPECTIVE PANORAMA of the METROPOLIS of England' was also taken from the top of the 'Albion Mills', though now from 'the ruins' rather than the entire building shown by the Barkers, and it consisted of an impressive 'Three Thousand Five Hundred square Feet of Canvas'. The selling point of the spectacle was its sheer scale, almost twice the size of the *Eidometropolis*, and this, the advertisements announced, creates an overwhelming impression of the magnitude of London and 'the mind of the spectator at once becomes impressed with the Idea that they are actually transported to the spot, amidst the hurry and bustle of this wonderful capital'.[63] The *Grand Perspective Panorama* has barely been noticed in the panorama literature and has not featured in discussions of either the Barkers' London views or Girtin's *Eidometropolis*, presumably because no visual evidence has been traced. We do, however, have the names of its creators. The Scottish landscape painter Alexander Nasmyth made the preparatory drawings and the canvas was painted by another Scot, the splendidly named scene painter, Cheap Cooper.[64] The *Grand Perspective Panorama* did not provide direct competition for the Girtins' spectacle, its tour keeping well away from the capital, but its significance for us lies in the way it highlights the problems the brothers faced. Touring outside the capital meant that a view familiar to a London audience might still feel new, even exotic, to spectators in a manner that Girtin's panorama could never match. The sheer scale of the canvas, set up in a specially constructed structure, also guaranteed a startling impact which Girtin could not hope to equal, however deceptive and artistically satisfying his view was. The *Eidometropolis* was simply under-capitalized, and in this company ill-equipped to compete as a popular spectacle.

Thomas Girtin, and latterly his brother John, too, may have made serious miscalculations regarding the *Eidometropolis* as a commercial venture, but, as the reviews made abundantly clear, the artistic credentials of the project were never in doubt. One crucial question remains, however, and it relates more specifically to the subject content of the panorama. Given that the *Eidometropolis* was a commercial failure, we need to investigate whether the artistic agenda compromised, indeed, was fundamentally incompatible with, the topographical subject and its accurate depiction. The best way to answer that question is to look at in more detail the visual evidence and the play between what was included in the 360-degree circle and how it was depicted.

CHAPTER THREE

London in seven sections: Girtin's topography traced

The six outline and five coloured drawings for the *Eidometropolis* that survive are of inestimable value, a unique combination of fine works of art and crucial evidence for understanding the original appearance of an early nineteenth-century panorama. The images are so arresting, however, that it is wise to preface an analysis of their subject content with a consideration of their shortcomings as evidence. The first point to make is that reproducing them in a book inevitably violates the fundamental principle of the panorama; namely, that in surrounding the viewer the original monumental canvas had no beginning or end. Laying out the two sets of drawings in a continuous strip (Fig. 30), with gaps for the missing images, shows how the drawings linked together, but it does so by introducing a false starting point. In this case, beginning with the larger right-hand part of the Albion Mills and proceeding clockwise has the advantage of prompting readers to imaginatively complete the circle by joining the left, undamaged portion of

the building in section seven, to the larger part in section one, but this is false to the panorama experience itself. It is possible that a *de facto* beginning was created in the *Eidometropolis*, since the entrance into the viewing circle from below must have presented the visitor with an initial prospect. Though there is no evidence of what that might have been, it is likely that the dramatic perspective of Blackfriars Bridge, with St Paul's rising above (Fig. 9), would have made a natural starting point for many spectators. The other note of caution required here is a reiteration of a point made earlier. The two sets of drawings were made in preparation for the painting of a circular canvas and are not, and could never have been, a record of the panorama's final appearance. The two series of seven views are the material from which another, very different object was created, and these sketches, in their use of traditional single point perspective and a landscape format, follow the same conventions as the artist's watercolours. It is worth looking at the

SECTION 1   SECTION 2   SECTION 3   SECTION 4

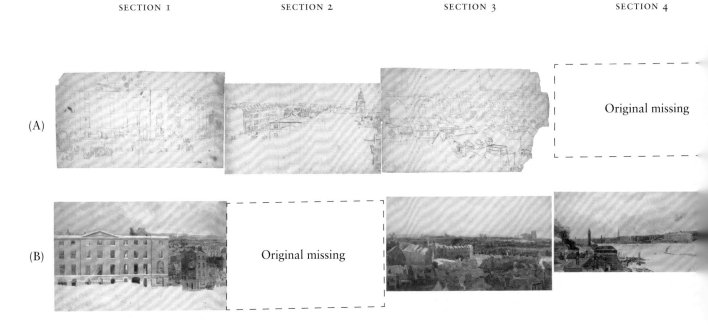

(A)

Original missing

(B)

Original missing

44

function of the drawings in more detail in order to understand the argument that what we are examining here are seven topographic views of London that were used to produce a single all-encompassing image that was fundamentally different.

From the outset Girtin adopted a different procedure from the earlier, half-circle, panoramic view from the Adelphi. There he produced three panoramic pencil studies, moving his angle of view on three occasions to create a continuous strip with three vanishing points (Figs 12–14). There is no grid and no evidence of the use of any drawing aid. Working from the roof of Albion Place Terrace on the outline views, however, Girtin reverted to the same proportions that he normally used in his watercolours, and this meant dividing the 360-degree field into seven sections. In contrast, Henry Aston Barker split his view of Paris into eight, making each section a convenient 45 degrees, but Girtin's preference for keeping to the format of his watercolours meant that his grid worked out at approximately 15½ squares (15.42 to be precise) or about 50 degrees (51.4) for each section, with each square on the grid covering a square foot on the canvas. This, not surprisingly, caused problems for his assistants when they came to transfer the outlines to the curved canvas since, as we shall see, the drawings do not complete the circle (Figs 10 and 1). Although there is no documentary evidence, Girtin's outlines are of such a uniform format and accuracy of detail that there is little doubt that, as with Henry Aston

Barker's surviving Paris drawings, a perspective frame was used in their production.[65] The frame would have had a grid of strings stretched across it, mirroring the grid on the paper in front of the artist, so that by keeping his head still Girtin could note down the relative positions of the architecture, together with their details, in an accurate and proportionate manner. Finishing one section, the artist would move the frame, and thus his angle of view, to begin the next on a separate sheet of paper of the same size and with the same grid.

The coloured drawings are of a different character as they were, despite their attractiveness as records of natural effects, not painted on the spot. Girtin began by copying, or perhaps even tracing, the outlines, though not the grid. Here he employed his characteristic textured laid cartridge paper, rather than the smooth wove papers used for the detailed outlines. Girtin then washed in, often very quickly and sometimes in a slapdash manner (Fig. 5), the predominant local colours and various light and weather effects. Some of the outlines contain annotations such as 'slates' or 'grass' (Fig. 4), suggesting that the intention from the outset was to colour the outlines from memory. It is possible that some colouring was added on the spot, but most, if not all, took place in the studio for the simple reason that it would have been impossible either to capture across seven sheets the complex range of transient atmospheric effects depicted in the coloured drawings or described in the textual

SECTION 5   SECTION 6   SECTION 7

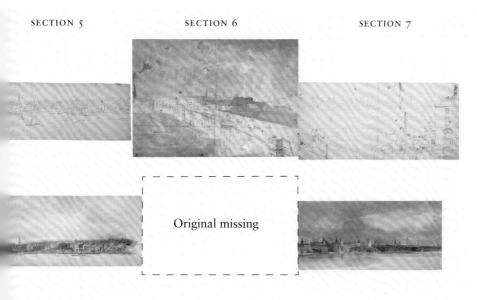

Original missing

Fig. 30   Composite strips of the surviving outline (A) and coloured drawings (B) madeby Thomas Girtin for the *Eidometropolis*.

sources, or to link them into the coherent harmonious whole praised by the critics. The fact that the *Eidometropolis* convinced as a snapshot of a moment across 360 degrees means that the preparatory coloured drawings, taking many hours to produce, could not have been executed on the roof of Albion Place Terrace. The sketchy manner of the colour application, which has been interpreted as evidence of their being made on the spot, is therefore a function of their role as models for others to work from, and the lack of detail suggests again the level of Girtin's involvement in the production of the canvas, akin to the master who worked only on the finishing details in a busy portrait painter's studio.

SECTION ONE
The Albion Mills, the View Looking South East

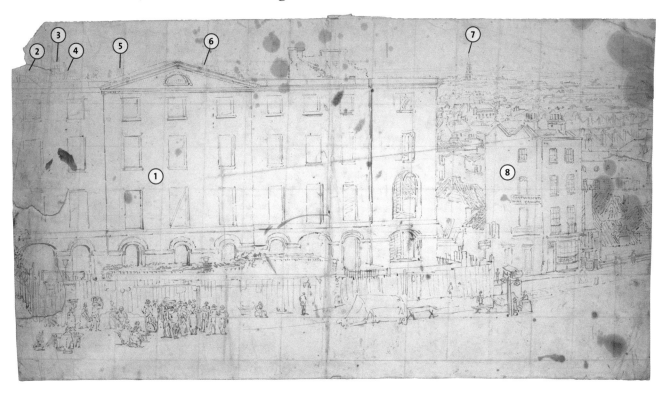

1 THE ALBION MILLS Built between 1783–86, the neo-classical structure housing the steam-powered mills was partially destroyed in a fire in March 1791.

2 ST OLAVE, TOOLEY STREET The square tower of 1740 is visible. The church was demolished in 1926.

3 ST SAVIOUR, SOUTHWARK The square tower of what was to become Southwark Cathedral is visible. At the time of Girtin's baptism there the building was in a poor state of preservation.

4 MAID MILL OR MAID LANE MILL Built on the roof of Skelton's Meeting House, it was demolished in 1820.

5 ST THOMAS, SOUTHWARK Built in 1702 on the site of the chapel of St Thomas' Hospital.

6 ST JOHN HORSLEYDOWN The building is one of those designated by the 1710 Act which stipulated the building of fifty new churches. It was built in 1727 and was designed by Nicholas Hawksmoor and John James.

7 ST GEORGE THE MARTYR, SOUTHWARK The church was rebuilt in 1734–36. It is in Borough High Street.

8 CARTWRIGHT'S WINE VAULT

Turning to the topographical content of Girtin's 'PICTURE of LONDON' one is immediately struck by the way in which the first section is dominated by one building to a degree unique in the 360-degree view, the burnt-out ruin of the Albion Mills (Figs 1–2). Girtin's viewpoint, from the Albion Place Terrace opposite, gave him a distinct advantage over the Barkers. They had the Albion Mills in their title, but the building itself was visible in its pre-ruined state only as an unsightly mass of roof, and the terrace from which Girtin took his view made for a dull foreground in comparison (Fig. 24). The view of the Albion Mills presented to Girtin was something of a mixed blessing, however. On the one hand, it came with a rich set of associations and a controversial history, on the other, the view, almost straight on, negated its picturesque potential, leading one reviewer to wish that the most prominent structure in the panorama had been 'more kept down in colour'.[66] Girtin's earlier watercolours of the interior of the ruined structure smouldering after the fire, made from the sketches of a local amateur artist, James Moore, show the sort of dramatic and sublime scene that the Mills might make (Fig. 31), but from a parallel position looking east the exterior of the structure resembles an architectural elevation. There are tantalizing glimpses through the monumental window openings of the confused mass of forms that makes the earlier

watercolour so interesting, but the panoramist has to record what is given and not what he knows to lie behind an elegant façade which bears no signs of its status as a contentious icon of industrial progress. Indeed, that is the point which is commonly forgotten. The architect, Samuel Wyatt, designed the western façade of the Albion Mills with its classical pediment so as to match the elegant domestic terrace opposite which he, and his brothers, had built in the 1770s as a commercial speculation.[67]

The construction and spectacular destruction of the Albion Mills was a major news story of the day, and few visitors to the *Eidometropolis* would not have had strong opinions on the subject. It was built between 1783 and 1786 to house the newly invented Boulton and Watt double-acting rotative engines which, it was promised to shareholders, would revolutionize the grinding of

Fig. 31   Thomas Girtin, *The Albion Mills after the Fire, c.* 1792, pencil and watercolour on paper, 18.9 × 22.7 cm, Newport Museum and Art Gallery (1940.22).

corn in the city. The three engines, driving thirty
pairs of stones, were expected to supplant the
wind-driven mills that still dotted the capital with
an industrial operation on an unprecedented
scale. The building itself was the most
technologically advanced structure of its time, as
well as being the most highly capitalized at over
£105,000. And even though technical problems
meant that the mills never ran to full capacity and
it made losses in many of its years in operation
up to the time of its destruction by fire in March
1791, it stood in the opinion of many as proof
of a 'triumphant technological progress'.[68]
Unsurprisingly, there was also considerable
opposition to the project from those whose
livelihoods were directly threatened or who saw
the downside of progress in more general terms.
Even though the fire was almost certainly begun
by the overheating of machinery on one of the
upper wooden floors, arson was widely sus-
pected, and the mob was shown celebrating the
conflagration in the popular prints of the day.
Even amongst more thoughtful commentators,
the monumental ruins, with their echoes in
Roman civic architecture, suggested a moral
lesson along the lines of the 'vanities of human
progress'.[69] Something of the latter may be
detected in Girtin's view, though probably it was
just fortuitous that one of Southwark's old-style
mills at Maid Lane is visible on the skyline to the
left of the building's pediment (Fig. 1).[70]

Immediately to the left of the mill, on the
horizon again, is the distinctive tower of St
Saviour, now Southwark Cathedral, which was
the scene of Girtin's baptism. The monumental
shell of Wyatt's neo-classical structure actually
obscures the district where the artist lived as a
child — he was born in the sadly lost Great
Bandy Leg Walk. The nearby Maid Mill,
variously described as a colour mill or a mill for
grinding bones, corn or gypsum, was
picturesquely located on the roof of Skelton's
Meeting House and was typical of the area's
small-scale industries, which were scattered
amongst the sort of humbler and anonymous
domestic accommodation occupied by the Girtin
family. According to George Griffin Stonestreet,
author of *Domestic Union, or London as it
Should Be!!* (published anonymously), this
'neglected and disparaged district' forms 'a Chaos
of dirty, crooked, narrow streets, lanes, allies and
laystalls, which it is impossible to explore without
regret and astonishment', though it did also
include 'a few opulent inhabitants'.[71] The traces
of smoke in the upper part of the coloured
drawing (Fig. 2) could come from any of the
larger manufactories located in the area,
including the Anchor Brewery, Potts's Vinegar
Works and the Falcon Glassworks, which are so
prominently displayed in the Barkers' panorama.
The irony of a burnt-out neo-classical building
obscuring a jumble of ramshackle, but working,
industries would no doubt have been savoured by
many viewers, especially as a number of schemes
to refurbish the ruins had failed to come to
fruition by the time Girtin came to depict his
native borough. Ten years after the fire, the ruins
remained behind a makeshift wooden fence to
keep out the crowds that passed through Albion
Place on their way to and from Blackfriars Bridge
and the City. Perhaps this was suitable location
for a prizefight after all, mirroring an earlier
conflict in the modernization of the area.

SECTION TWO
Great Surrey Street and Christ Church, Southwark, the View Looking South

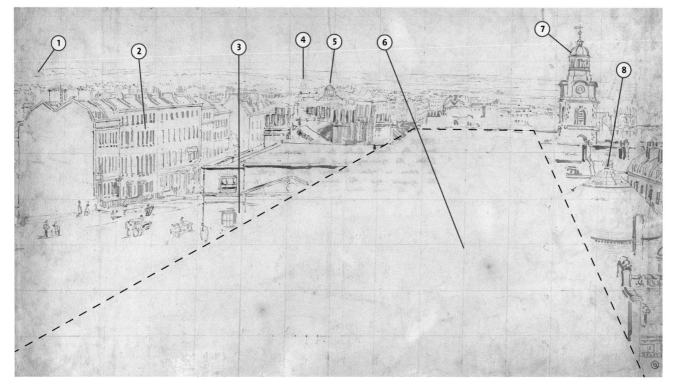

1 KING'S BENCH PRISON   The large structure (built 1758) is viewed from side on and cannot be distinguished on the outline drawing.

2 GREAT SURREY STREET   The street was built after the completion of Blackfriars Bridge in 1769. It changed its name to Blackfriars Road in 1829.

3 CROSS KEYS COFFEE HOUSE

4 ST MARY, NEWINGTON   The eighteenth-century building was demolished in 1876.

5 THE SURREY CHAPEL   The circular, non-denominational chapel, opened in 1783, was built for the Evangelical preacher, Rowland Hill (1744–1833).

6 THE ROOF AND CHIMNEYS OF ALBION PLACE TERRACE The four-storey terrace was built in the 1770s by the architect/engineer of Albion Mills, Samuel Wyatt. The blank area within the dotted outline was mocked up as a three-dimensional structure.

7 CHRIST CHURCH, SOUTHWARK   The church was rebuilt between 1738–41 with a three-storey clock tower. It was demolished after being damaged in the Second World War.

8 THE ROTUNDA, SIR ASHTON LEVER'S MUSEUM OF NATURAL CURIOSITIES   The round room was opened in 1789 as the focal point of the display. The Museum closed in 1806.

The view south east in section one includes an area of the countryside that lay beyond London's expanding boundaries, and this continues into the next scene which shows the southern vista (Fig. 3). The coloured drawing for section two has not been located, but it, too, would have been dominated by the area left blank in the foreground here. Relating Figures 24 and 29 to the outline, it is possible to establish Girtin's viewpoint as being from the river end of the roof of the four-storey Albion Place Terrace. The blank space in the outline was therefore occupied by the receding length of the roof and four sets of chimneys, and this would have obscured much of the buildings to the immediate left and right, the Cross Keys Coffee House and the Rotunda of the Leverian Museum of Natural Curiosities. The shallower recession of the roof to the left indicates that Girtin took up a position to its right. This large stretch was presumably left blank in the drawing because it would not have been possible to paint such close objects in an illusive manner on the canvas and the roof would have been mocked up instead as a three-dimensional structure, using real tiles and chimneys as a way of reinforcing the impression that the spectator was standing on the spot that Girtin had occupied. This is confirmed by an account of the 'person who attends the visitors' and who, in order to 'determine a dispute whether some earthen chimney-pots that are on one of the houses, were three or four feet long [...] proved them to be no more than six inches!'.[72] The master of perspective, it is implied, could confuse spectators even if they had the real thing as a comparison.

The Barkers' earlier London panorama contained an even greater roof area, and such obstacles were inevitable for a panoramist who did not want to adopt a bird's-eye view which, though it might depict a greater extent, looked down from such a distance that the viewer loses any attachment to the subject.[73] The view from the Albion Place Terrace was not perfect in this respect, but the vista south was not the most interesting topographically or pictorially. Indeed, the area had rarely been depicted, being the result primarily of recent building work following the completion of Blackfriars Bridge in 1769. Many of the earliest panoramic views of London may have been taken from the riverbank here, looking north, but the artists had literally turned their backs to the less developed south. Wenceslaus Hollar's six-sheet *Prospect from Whitehall to Greenwich* (1647) and Samuel and Nathaniel Buck's *Prospect of London and Westminster* (1749), for instance, both visualized London primarily as an extended view of the north bank of the river as it snaked through the metropolis, the latter taken from four different viewpoints.[74] Indeed, there is a strong correlation between the development of the panorama and the building up of London south of the river. The subsequent urbanization of the capital means that the city completed its own 360-degree circuit in the decades following the introduction of the new spectacle, and Girtin's sections one to three effectively filled in the circle left incomplete in the older panoramic views. Viewed from Blackfriars Bridge, the catalyst for the new developments, Girtin's views of London south of the river were inevitably dominated by evidence of the city's dynamic expansion. The distant fields and hills in these sectors, showing the villages of Sydenham, Dulwich and Norwood, are amongst the most prominent rural expanses in the *Eidometropolis*. The expansion of the city had not yet reached this far, but the powerful perspective of the terraces that line Great Surrey Street, mirroring the bold form of Blackfriars Bridge opposite, emphasize the forward march of progress and, as one newspaper noted, the *Eidometropolis* would as a result be of particular interest to the 'Antiquary' of the future who 'would see what London was, and mark the great alterations that are about to take place'.[75]

The author was thinking of the changes proposed for around London Bridge at this date, but for others it was the rapid expansion of the city into the 'Surrounding Country' that arrested their attention. London seen 'from an exalted situation', claimed another notice of Girtin's view, 'commands admiration equal to the astonishment of strangers in perambulating the vast increasing extent of the metropolis', and the sense of the city's growth receives its most powerful expression in this section.[76]

As Girtin's earlier panoramic drawing made from the Adelphi demonstrates, the logic of the extended view dictates that, for every section which approximates to the balanced compositions favoured by topographers intent on showing architectural subjects at their best, other less favourable views open up as a consequence. In this case, the frontal view of the Albion Mills in the previous section is succeeded here by an undistinguished jumble where no building is shown complete and an undue prominence is given to run-of-the-mill terraces, a featureless flat roof and a plethora of chimneys, whilst the nearby three-storey clock tower of Christ Church, Southwark, looms larger than the dome of St Paul's in the opposite section. Christ Church, like the majority of the buildings in this section, was relatively new, being completed in 1741 and, although by no means an insignificant monument, it had none of the architectural pretensions of Sir Christopher Wren's City churches.[77] This was even more the case with the Surrey Chapel, the cupola of which appears to the left. The chapel was built for the charismatic preacher the Revd Rowland Hill and opened in 1783 in what was then an underdeveloped area. The unusual circular structure was the subject of a number of prints, but this was more because it provided a welcoming space for a large congregation than for any architectural merits it possessed. What was perhaps the best-known landmark in an otherwise barren landscape for topographers appears to the bottom right of Girtin's view, the extensive rotunda that was built in 1788–89 to add a dramatic conclusion for the suite of rooms that housed Sir Ashton Lever's Museum of Natural Curiosities. The entrance to the museum can be seen in the corresponding section of the Barkers' panorama, which depicts the other side of Great Surrey Street. But, from Girtin's viewpoint, the smart set of rooms developed by the owner of the collection, James Parkinson, is represented by the utilitarian exterior of the round structure, the roof of which was noted by Girtin as being in 'slate', with the central light marked 'glass'. The collection was originally housed in the central location for such amusements, Leicester Square, and its new home south of the river was not a success. What was described as 'London's most complete cabinet of natural curiosities' failed to attract enough visitors to this marginal situation and it closed in 1806.[78] At least in this respect the Girtins did not make such a miscalculation, siting the *Eidometropolis* in Spring Gardens, near to what was even then the heart of London's entertainment district.

SECTION THREE
Lambeth and Westminster, the View Looking South West

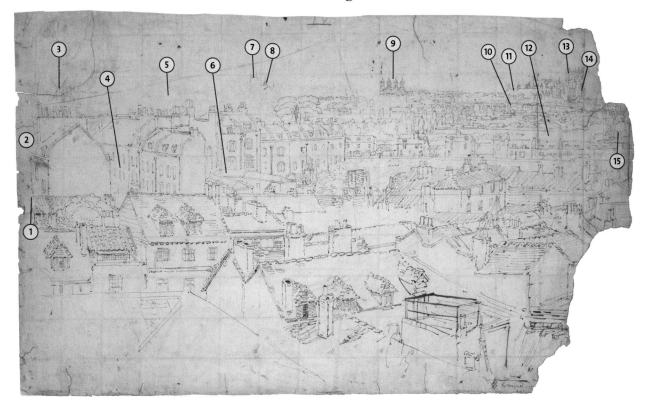

1 UPPER GROUND   Older housing on the road running parallel to the river.

2 STAMFORD STREET   The eastern end of terrace housing was built *c.* 1790 and was extended *c.* 1803 to meet Broad Wall.

3 NEW CUT WINDMILL

4 BENNETT STREET

5 LAMBETH WINDMILLS   There were at least three mills in this area. One of the two shown here is the Apothecary's Mill

6 UNIDENTIFIED HORSESHOE-SHAPED BUILDING Nothing of this description appears on Horwood's contemporary map.

7 ST MARY-AT-LAMBETH   The church and tower were built 1374–78 next to Lambeth Palace.

8 THE GREAT HALL, LAMBETH PALACE   Pragnell suggests that the smaller tower here is the louvre of the Great Hall.

9 ST JOHN, SMITH SQUARE   Designed by Thomas Archer and completed in 1728. Known as Queen Anne's Footstool with its four corner towers.

10 WESTMINSTER BRIDGE   Designed by the Swiss architect Charles Labelye, it was built between 1739–50 with fifteen arches constructed in Portland stone.

11 WESTMINSTER HALL   The only surviving part of the original Palace of Westminster.

12 TENTER GROUNDS   Used by the Woollen Cloth Manufactory located next to the Patent Shot Manufactory.

13 WESTMINSTER ABBEY   Begun in the thirteenth century, the nave was finished in the fourteenth century and the west towers, to a design by Nicholas Hawksmoor, were completed in 1745.

14 ST MARGARET, WESTMINSTER   The church was rebuilt between 1486 and 1523 and is the parish church for the House of Commons. The church was refaced in Portland stone and the tower rebuilt in 1734.

15 BROAD WALL   This was the boundary of Lambeth Marsh and is marked by a line of older housing.

The next section (Figs 4–5), showing the view south west over Lambeth towards Westminster, also includes evidence of recent developments with a sunlit stretch of new terraces dominating the middle ground. In this section, though, the straight lines and regular forms of the newly constructed properties are contrasted with three distinct areas which together constitute the most complex interaction of different periods and contrasting land uses seen in the *Eidometropolis*. The foreground is thus dominated by an older mix of housing and small-scale workshops and industries that back up from the river, and this leads into another line of older dwellings, the Broad Wall, which marked the old ditch boundary of Lambeth Marsh. Prior to the opening of Waterloo Bridge in 1817, Lambeth was still predominantly rural in character, and it appears in Girtin's coloured drawing as an expanse of trees, market gardens and tenter grounds beyond the newly built Stamford Terrace. And then, further on, Westminster on the horizon features some of the capital's most venerable historic monuments and a glimpse of the riverbank, too.

These disparate elements are linked by broad areas of sunlight, with the short shadows indicating that Girtin chose noon or just after as his time of day. Section one is also illuminated by strong, even sunlight, and so presumably was the missing coloured drawing for the second section, confirming what the reviews identified as a clear division in the 360-degree canvas between the northern part of the city with mixed skies and stormy effects and sunnier weather south of the river. There is no evidence that this was interpreted as holding a particular significance, rather that it demonstrated the artist's masterly ability to depict contrasting effects whilst 'the whole is in harmony'.[79] Girtin had the confidence to illuminate some of the least attractive areas of his scene, at the same time as casting great monuments such as Westminster Abbey into relative gloom and saving the boldest effects for one section to the north which actually requires less help pictorially.

The question of what time of the day is depicted in the *Eidometropolis* is worth considering here since selecting midday, or just after, makes it look as though Girtin, as with his choice of a calm river surface, passed up an opportunity to enhance the drama of his view. However, as Ann Bermingham has recently argued, the format of the panorama made the choice of an even,

midday light, all but inevitable.[80] The sun at dusk or dawn might have created more interesting, warm-toned effects, but then the sun, lower to the horizon, would have had to be depicted on the canvas, shining into the eyes of the spectator. And then it must be remembered that the canvas was itself lit from above, with light filtered through a gauze suspended under the sort of glass roof which crowned the Rotunda of the Leverian Museum seen in section two (Fig. 3). Anything other than a midday effect would have contradicted the actual light source of the canvas, therefore. The smoke, too, in this section rises close to the vertical, suggesting little wind, and there is nothing in the other landscape elements to persuade viewers that they are observing anything other than a calm midsummer day.

As in the second section, this view is dominated by a brightly lit, recently built terrace, in this case driving a wedge between the ramshackle collection of older houses and workshops with their smoky chimneys that lined Upper Ground in the foreground and the largely undeveloped part of Lambeth beyond. The newly built terraces along Stamford Street, dating from about 1790, with another range in Bennet Street approaching us at right angles, advances towards the old line of housing at Broad Wall. The new terraces were built in London stock bricks with slate roofs, but it was not just the symmetrical form and distinctive use of building materials which contrast them with the picturesque irregularity of the clay-tiled roofs of the pre-1774 Building Act accommodation in the foreground.[81] The three-storey terraces, with their mansard roofs and dormers, are divided by prominent interior party walls which stand proud above. The windows, too, are recessed as part of the efforts to improve fire safety which drove the Act, and this feature can be deduced from the slim shadows which appear around them. Stamford Street was in the vanguard in this part of London of the increase in speculative building which, by conforming to the new regulations, tended to produce a dull uniformity when seen *en masse*.[82] This appealed to proponents of the rational improvement of the city, but appalled those who saw speculative building as the naked pursuit of profit. Such was the quickening pace of change in this area that, even before the *Eidometropolis* closed to the public in the middle of 1803, Stamford Terrace was extended to form Upper Stamford Street, marking another stage in the march of development into under-populated areas. And with such developments went the district's tenter grounds, the areas of open space used to dry newly manufactured cloth which adjoined the last vestiges of that industry before it relocated completely to the northern counties. One part of the coloured drawing (Fig. 5), which is marked on Girtin's outline as 'grass' (Fig. 4), has a series of white areas created by leaving the paper untouched and they presumably represent cloth drying in the sun.

There is enough detail in Girtin's coloured drawing for us to appreciate the rural quality of the landscape beyond Stamford Street that was partly obscured to the viewers of the panorama by the new developments. Numerous market gardens interspersed with trees, many of which were features in the old pleasure gardens at Cuper's Bridge noticed in the earlier view from the Adelphi (Fig. 13), are relieved towards the horizon by no less than three windmills. They offer more than a thematic contrast with the industrialized mill in the opening section, however, as they also signify that this area was essentially rural in character. City mills were invariably located next to the water, or, as here, built in areas where there were no tall buildings to disrupt the wind flow. Old windmills are notoriously difficult to identify, but the example to the left is clearly the New Cut Mill which appears in many other local views, including the Barkers' panorama. One of the two mills to the right is the Apothecary's Mill, which features in a number of watercolours by Paul Sandby.[83] Silhouetted on the skyline, the three humble mills are granted a democratic equality with the parish's historically significant buildings, including the barely discernible tower of St Mary-at-Lambeth and the indistinct roof of the Great Hall of Lambeth Palace.

The historic buildings to the east of Lambeth over the river may be more distinct, but their appearance is severely compromised by the arbitrary alignments that the panorama generates here. The isolated and distinctive profile of St John Smith Square is fine, but Westminster Abbey, Westminster Hall and St Margaret, Westminster,

all merge into one confused mass of Gothic forms and the arches of Westminster Bridge below are interrupted by the jumble of anonymous industrial buildings on the south bank. As the critics explained, this area highlighted two interrelated problems inherent in city panoramas. The first, as the Paris correspondent of *London und Paris* complained, was that whilst Girtin's viewpoint may have been perfect for the 'magnificent and famous St Paul's', the ancient buildings of Westminster 'can only be seen from a distance and thus not entirely clearly'; indeed, they are 'virtually unrecognizable'.[84] The success of the panorama in creating an illusive experience actually draws attention in other areas to the impossibility of dealing satisfactorily with the topographic content as a whole. An otherwise supportive writer in the *Monthly Magazine* developed the critique, noting that the 'two towers of Westminster-abbey appear in one mass, which destroys that lightness and air which constitute a leading beauty in the building'. Missing the point of a panorama which seeks to place the spectator on the same spot as the artist, he added that, though from 'the point of view in which it is taken it is probably a true represent-ation [...] a license is allowed to painters [...] and where a picturesque effect can be produced, a trifling deviation would [...] be overlooked, or forgiven', forgetting that he had just criticized the artist for showing Westminster Bridge 'to be more circular than it is in nature'.[85] Section three exemplifies the radical nature of the relationship between the panorama and its ostensible subject matter on two counts, therefore. In the first instance, it repeatedly inverts the subject hier-archy, presenting the humble dwelling in the foreground in intimate detail with the great buildings of state and church relegated to the distance. And in the second, it takes the familiar and the famous and, as chance dictates, distorts, occludes and defaces it. The 'grandeur of Westminster Abbey' promised in one of Girtin's advertisements is hopelessly compromised by a spectacle where the topographical subject can be equally well or badly served.[86]

SECTION FOUR

The Thames from Westminster to Somerset House, the View Looking West

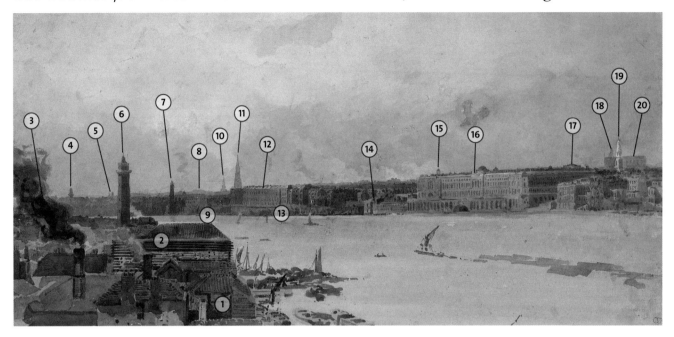

1 LUKIN'S IRON FOUNDRY This is identified in advertisements as the company of James Lukin & Co.

2 NICHOLSON'S TIMBER YARD F. Nicholson, timber and deal merchant is listed in trade directories.

3 THE BANQUETING HOUSE, WHITEHALL This is obscured by the smoke from the iron foundry.

4 HORSE GUARDS, WHITEHALL The barracks were designed by William Kent and built 1750–59. It is the clock tower which can be seen here.

5 THE TELEGRAPH ON THE ADMIRALTY OFFICE, CHARING CROSS Erected in 1796, the shutter telegraph initiated four routes, signalling to Portsmouth, Plymouth, Deal and Yarmouth.

6 PATENT SHOT TOWER (WATT'S SHOT TOWER) The world's first shot tower was built in 1789 and was forty-two metres high, the lead shot falling thirty-seven metres. The inventor was William Watt.

7 THE WATER TOWER, YORK BUILDINGS The works were the first to use steam power with a 'machine for raising water by fire', in 1712. The octagonal tower measured seventy metres high.

8 THE KING'S THEATRE, HAYMARKET The theatre was rebuilt in 1791 to a design by Michael Novosielski and was the largest in Britain.

9 YORK WATERGATE

10 ST JAMES, PICCADILLY Built from a design by Wren between 1676–84, the lead-covered spire visible here dates from 1699–1700.

11 ST MARTIN-IN-THE-FIELDS Rebuilt by James Gibbs, 1722–26. The spire rises to fifty-nine metres and from this angle appears to merge into the Adelphi Terrace.

12 THE ADELPHI TERRACE The first great Georgian riverside development, projected by Robert, James and William Adam (Adelphi is Greek for brothers). The forty-one bays of the Royal Terrace dominated the bend of the river. Building began in 1768 with the first tenants arriving in 1772.

13 THE ADELPHI WHARFS The wharfs underneath the luxury apartments were the commercial bedrock of the project and were used at this time by coal merchants in particular.

14 THE RUINS OF THE SAVOY PALACE The ruins, barely visible here, were sketched by the young Girtin and his contemporary J. M. W. Turner. The medieval ruins were swept away to create the approach to Waterloo Bridge, opened in 1817.

15 ST PAUL, COVENT GARDEN The small cupola peeks above the western arm of Somerset House. Girtin was buried here in November 1802.

16 SOMERSET HOUSE Work began with the Strand front of nine bays, 1776–80, and the river front was still incomplete when Girtin's panorama was painted. William Chambers's design housed numerous public bodies and was the most important building project of its day. The shallow dome, much criticized for its timid appearance, appears in the middle of the skyline and the clock tower

of the western range is to the right. The river, as yet unembanked, flowed up to its monumental arcades.

17 COVENT GARDEN THEATRE The auditorium was reshaped by Henry Holland, but it burnt down in 1808.

18 ST GILES-IN-THE-FIELDS Designed by Henry Flitcroft and built 1731–33. The steeple appears behind Drury Lane Theatre.

19 ST MARY-LE-STRAND Designed by James Gibbs and built in Portland stone between 1714–17, this was one of the fifty new churches promised by the 1710 Act.

20 DRURY LANE THEATRE The cavernous theatre, accommodating more than 3,600 spectators, was the result of a rebuild masterminded by Henry Holland and opened in 1794. It burnt down in 1809.

The only drawing that has survived for section four is a coloured drawing (Fig. 6) which looks to the west, and although it has been cut at the bottom the striking industrial foreground still dominates, explaining why this area attracted the particular attention of those critics who appreciated Girtin's innovative approach to the panorama. The *Morning Herald*, for instance, requested its readers to 'take notice of the smoak floating across the picture from Lukin's Foundry' in the same line that it recommended the 'grandeur of St Paul's'.[87] The *Monthly Magazine*, in turn, singled out the manner in which 'the view towards the east appears through a sort of misty medium, arising from the fires of the forges, manufactories, &c. which gradually lessens as we survey the western extremity', claiming this a good 'example' of the way that Girtin 'paid particular attention to representing the objects of the hue with which they appear in nature, and, by that means, greatly heighten the illusion'.[88] The description of the way that the smoky effect 'gradually lessens' is not borne out by the coloured drawings for sections three and four, however (Figs 5 and 6). As the composite strip of the colour sketches illustrates (Fig. 30), there is gap between the two, suggesting that the drawing for section three (Fig. 5) was slightly cut down, but this is not enough to account for the abrupt termination of the smoke at the edge of this sheet. The smoke from the foundry, if carried on to its natural extent, would not just have obscured the Banqueting House but Westminster Abbey, too, and that would have taken the emphasis on natural effects too far. The subtle way that the smoke 'gradually lessens' was presumably improvised on the canvas by Girtin himself so as to leave historic Westminster at least partly visible.

As we have seen with Girtin's depiction of the south bank further upriver (Fig. 13), it is not easy to identify the industrial buildings along the Thames. But Girtin helps viewers by including part of the sign for 'Lukins' iron foundry, and the adjacent buildings were also represented by other

artists, with one watercolour by an anonymous amateur depicting the same sequence of foundry, Nicholson's timber yard and the Patent Shot Tower.[89] The Shot Tower, in particular, appears in numerous views (Fig. 18).[90] Nicholson's timber yard, with a similar gathering of London sailing barges around its wharf, also features in many depictions of Blackfriars Bridge. Significantly, none of these views make use of the picturesque possibilities of smoke in the way that was advocated by James Malcolm in his contemporary account of the city, *Londinium Redivivum*. Malcolm's watercolour of the Water Tower on the north bank at York Buildings (Fig. 17), visible in this section of Girtin's view to the right of the Shot Tower, includes smoke emerging from the engine that pumped the water up the 70 metre-high tower, but in the text he went much further. Smoke may be 'an enemy to prospects', he began, but as 'the everlasting companion of this great city' it is also 'emblematic of its magnificence'. On 'a calm day', he continued, note how it is 'pleasing to observe the black streams which issue from the different manufactories; sometimes darting upward, while every trifling current gives graceful undulations; at others rolling in slow movements, blending with the common mass'.[91] As John Brewer has suggested, smoke 'was an enemy to prospects' because it was only for a few hours on the clearest days that every building might be seen clearly, but Girtin was not intent on producing a lucid and even depiction of everything within his view.[92] Smoke from any number of sources, not just Lukin's Foundry, was a fundamental part of the city, even on a summer's day, and for an artist who wished to show 'London, in a picturesque way', or even as a 'sublime' spectacle, Girtin had a potent resource at his command.

The contrast between the south and north banks of the Thames at this point could not be sharper, with the latter dominated by the monumental classical form of the river front of Somerset House, the major public building project of the day. Although predominantly in shade, the

Portland stone façade stands out, though there are also signs that the building, after a quarter of a century, was still not complete. The eastern flank, built in brick because it was not designed to be visible, can be seen all too clearly, and the façade terminates well short of its planned width. Designed by Sir William Chambers to be symmetrical, work had slowed down amidst much criticism, and in 1801 it still lacked a flanking pediment and six bays to the east. The Thames in its unembanked state was then much wider at this point, and the river is shown at high tide flowing up to the monumental arcade which supports the building's terrace with the semicircular arch in the centre providing access to storage space below. The sheer scale of the edifice, its monumental classical idiom and its rich use of stone all offer a telling contrast with the site from which Girtin made his earlier panoramic drawing, the Adelphi Terrace. The brick façade of the building barely emerges from the gloom that predominates here, turning major landmarks such as the spire of St Martin-in-the-Fields into broad silhouettes and rendering the picturesque remains of the medieval Savoy Palace all but invisible. These ruins, which were said to be the subject of the youthful Girtin's earliest landscape sketches, are located midway between the twin modern developments that initiated the transformation of the old *ad hoc* mix of small-scale buildings and gardens into an imposing riverside suited to the capital of an imperial power.

A view from Blackfriars Bridge gives no sense of the rapid expansion of the capital to the west, and the new squares and terraces that were its most characteristic architectural feature are not visible in this section. But modern London left its mark north of the river in the form of what, after Somerset House, were the largest public buildings of their day, a new generation of monumental theatres erected in the 1790s. The formless bulk of the Drury Lane Theatre, rebuilt in 1792, looms to the right of Chambers's great public work, with Covent Garden Theatre, opened in 1794, to its left. A third, even larger, auditorium appears on the horizon to the right of the York Water Works, the King's Theatre, Haymarket. But perhaps the most intriguing addition to the skyline in this section, and certainly the most

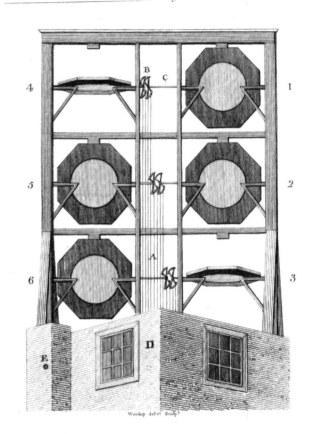

View *of the* TELEGRAPH *on the Admiralty.*

Fig. 32 Anonymous, *View of the Telegraph on the Admiralty*, c. 1800, etching, 15.1 × 9.8 cm, British Museum, London (1880,1113.2781.3).

recent, appears immediately to the left of the Shot Tower. From the advertisements for Cooper and Nasmyth's *Grand Perspective Panorama* it is possible to identify the twin vertical forms here as the 'Telegraph on the Admiralty' (Fig. 32). This was erected in 1796 on the Admiralty Office, Charing Cross, and is therefore the only sign in the *Eidometropolis* that, even as work began on the canvas, Britain was at war with France. The signalling system consisted of two frames with six shutters which could be opened and closed to form the code for each of the letters of the alphabet, and this was visible at a distance of up to 13 kilometres.

SECTION FIVE

The Thames from the Temple to Blackfriars, the View Looking North West

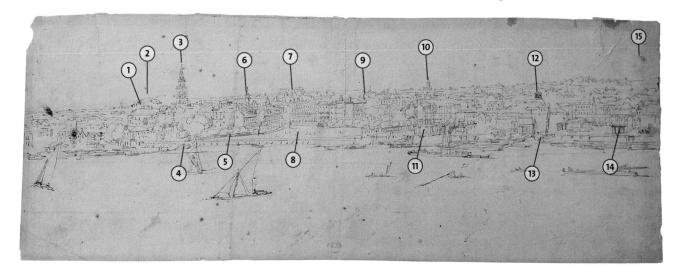

1 FREEMASON'S HALL   Designed by Thomas Sandby and built 1775–76. The mass of buildings here may also include the more distant British Museum.

2 ST GEORGE, BLOOMSBURY   Designed by Nicholas Hawksmoor, the distinctive tower (1729–31) is crowned with a statue of George I.

3 ST CLEMENT DANES, THE STRAND   The prominent steeple was the work of James Gibb who added to Wren's tower in 1719.

4 MIDDLE TEMPLE STAIRS

5 MIDDLE TEMPLE GARDENS

6 MIDDLE TEMPLE HALL   The finest Elizabethan building in central London.

7 LINCOLN'S INN   The formless mass here appears to be the Hall of Lincoln's Inn, one of the four Inns of Court.

8 INNER TEMPLE GARDENS   They were laid out in 1601.

9 TEMPLE CHURCH   The top of the circular nave with its crenellations is visible above the newer buildings of the Inner Temple.

10 ST DUNSTAN-IN-THE-WEST   The medieval church on Fleet Street was demolished and rebuilt 1830–33.

11 GRAND JUNCTION WHARF

12 WHITEFRIARS GLASS HOUSE

13 WHITEFRIARS DOCKS

14 NEW RIVER OFFICE   The New River Company was founded in the early seventeenth century to bring fresh water into the city. The grand office was designed by Colen Campbell.

15 ST ANDREW, HOLBORN   The medieval tower was refaced in Portland stone in 1703 and heightened.

The broken sky in section four picks out a few highlights in what is otherwise a cloudy, sometimes gloomy effect, and whilst this continues into section five, the predominant effect in the view from the Temple to Blackfriars, looking north west (Fig. 8), is of a bright noonday sun with the clouds occasionally parting to light up the west and south-facing walls of the buildings and open spaces which face the river. The relatively simple composition here with the main buildings placed obliquely to the river in a narrow band, combined with the sparsity of significant landmarks, echoes the middle section of the earlier panoramic drawing of the south bank (Fig. 13) in that everything is concentrated into a narrow strip with a large part of the river omitted. The sunny effect on the oasis of green of the Temple Gardens in the centre was noticed by the *Monthly Magazine* which praised the 'brighter tint' that gave way to the storm that was gathering over the City.[93] Indeed, the Girtins stressed the importance of the Temple Gardens in their advertisements, including them in a relatively short list of the most significant sites. However, it was their historical associations that presumably rendered the site important, rather than the position of the gardens at the centre of one of the four Inns of Court. It was in the Inner Temple Gardens, as they are more correctly known, that, according to Shakespeare in *Henry VI, Part I*, the Wars of the Roses had their origin. Behind, the bold form of the Middle Temple Hall rises up. Built between 1562 and 1573, this is perhaps the finest Elizabethan building in central

London, measuring over 30 metres long with an 18 metre-high hammerbeam roof, and it was famously the location of the first performance of *Twelfth Night*, with Shakespeare himself playing a role. The rich historical associations continue with the appearance of the Temple Church, dating from 1161. The circular nave of the church, with its distinctive crenellations, is picked out by sunlight emerging from the shadows of the newer buildings of the Inner Temple. The characteristic circular form of churches associated with the Templars paid homage to Christ's sepulchre.

There is no suggestion that Girtin used the sunlight to simply highlight important historical buildings, however. The band of light thus extends further east to include a group of commercial properties and wharves, stretching from the monumental warehouse at the Grand Junction Wharf to the New River Office just before Blackfriars Bridge, taking in Whitefriars Docks, with the Whitefriars Glasshouse behind.[94] This is the corollary to the arbitrary cut-offs and alignments that occur across the panorama. The characteristic light effects with which the artist invested the composition with variety and contrast can invert the subject hierarchy too. The need for a bright accent to set off 'the impending storm over the City' in the next section means not only that this commercial area is lit up with the same intensity as one of the legal centres of the capital, but also that it is rendered in more detail and with a greater impact than more intrinsically interesting stretches of the riverbank, both east and west.[95] The storm over the City (Fig. 11) renders details of its commercial and trading

activity comparatively invisible where they were actually most intense.

The recent discovery of the outline drawing for this section (Fig. 7) has thrown up an intriguing problem with important implications for our understanding of the production of the *Eidometropolis*. A prominent feature of the coloured drawing is the large warehouse at the Grand Junction Wharf, immediately to the east of the Inner Temple Gardens, but this is not present in the outline drawing. The same area is occupied by a row of columns and what appears to be scaffolding. In other words the outline seems to show the warehouse at an early stage of its construction, presenting us with two possible scenarios. Either Girtin made the coloured drawing some time after the outline, possibly a year or so later, or he imagined what the incomplete building would look like in the future and made this a prominent feature of the coloured drawing and subsequently the finished canvas itself. The significant delay between the completion of the canvas in 1801 and its showing the next year suggests a further option, however. Could it be that the coloured drawing actually records a later reworking of the canvas which brought it up to date for its opening in August 1802? Frustratingly, it has not been possible to establish the precise dates of the construction of the warehouse, but it does seem likely that in this section of the panorama at least, Girtin responded to, and recorded London's constantly changing face and that this characteristically took the form of an expansion in the city's trading infrastructure.

SECTION SIX
Blackfriars Bridge and St Paul's Cathedral, the View Looking North

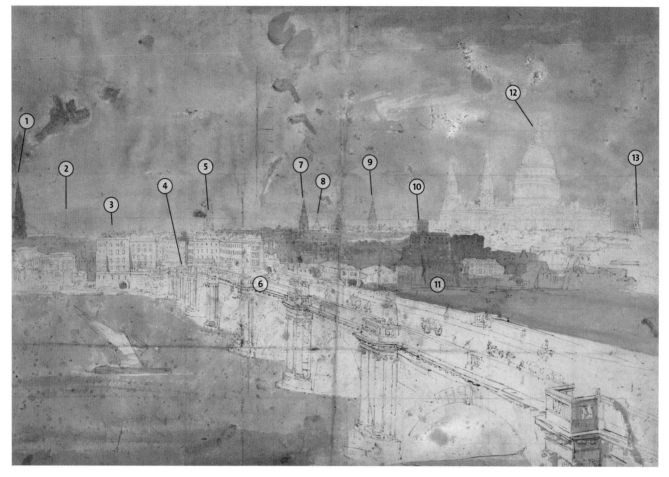

1 ST BRIDE, FLEET STREET The spire, consisting of four octagonal arcades of diminishing size, was added to Wren's church in 1701–03. It is sixty-nine metres high.

2 ST JAMES, CLERKENWELL The church was rebuilt between 1788–92 by James Carr.

3 THE CHAPEL, BRIDEWELL PRISON

4 CHATHAM PLACE

5 ST SEPULCHRE-WITHOUT-NEWGATE The distinctive tower was rebuilt 1630–34 and restored after the Great Fire.

6 BLACKFRIARS BRIDGE Designed by Robert Mylne, the bridge, consisting of nine semi-elliptical Portland stone arches, was built between 1760–69. Tolls were scrapped in 1785.

7 ST MARTIN LUDGATE The church was rebuilt by Wren (1677–86) with a lead steeple mounted on a lead-covered cupola.

8 ROYAL COLLEGE OF PHYSICIANS The octagonal dome housed the anatomy theatre, opened in 1679. It was probably designed by Robert Hooke.

9 CHRIST CHURCH, GREYFRIARS Wren replaced the medieval church after the Great Fire, 1677–87. Only the tower now remains.

10 ST ANDREW-BY-THE-WARDROBE The church was rebuilt by Wren in 1685–95.

11 PUDDLE DOCK The dock is in front of the square tower of St Andrew's.

12 ST PAUL'S CATHEDRAL The construction of Wren's masterpiece proceeded from east to west with the choir completed by 1702, the west towers were built 1705–08, and the dome was finished in 1708. The Portland-stone building measures 155 metres long and the top of the lantern is 111 metres from the ground.

13 ST AUGUSTINE, WATLING STREET The church was rebuilt by Wren (1680–84) after the Great Fire with a steeple probably designed by Hawksmoor. Only the tower remains.

The connection between sections five and six (Figs 8 and 9), is unique in two respects. The coloured drawing for section five firstly peters out at the edge and, secondly, the link itself is the subject of a separate small pencil study (Fig. 33) which includes architectural details of the steeple of St Bride's church that are obscured by the grey washes added to the outline drawing.[96] The coloured drawing for this section has not been located, but it would have played a significant role in the production of the final canvas as it features such a complex effect, an 'impending storm', which reviewers thought complemented Sir Christopher Wren's masterpiece, St Paul's Cathedral. Indeed, an early sale of Girtin's works included no less than three drawings of the bridge.[97] The cathedral rose with 'the most majestic dignity above all the surrounding buildings', wrote one critic, and its setting had about it the 'grandeur' that the Girtins promised in their advertisements.[98] Unlike the disorderly form of Westminster Abbey, enough of the west façade, the western spires, the southern transept and the monumental dome were visible to convey the cathedral's overwhelming scale, and Girtin's viewpoint was calculated to show off its architectural merits to the full. Wren's triumph, which was declared finished in 1711, was widely regarded as a potent symbol of London and its

miraculous regeneration after the Great Fire of 1666. As William Coombe noted in his *History of the River Thames* (1796), this 'stupendous fabric [...] is the pride of his country, and has ranked him among the first men that have adorned the world'.[99] A stormy setting therefore reinforced the building's symbolic status as a monument to British steadfastness, and it was no doubt with this section in mind that the *Morning Herald* characterized the particular attraction of Girtin's panorama in strident patriotic terms, claiming that 'every Briton and lover of his country' will stand 'enraptured [...] in seeing his native place, the glory of the world, so finely and truly pourtrayed'.[100]

The juxtaposition of the classical idiom of the cathedral and that of Robert Mylne's Blackfriars Bridge, built 1760–69, added another level of meaning to Girtin's *Eidometropolis*. The graceful curve of the bridge, with its nine monumental stone arches divided by pairs of elegant classical columns, appears to support the bulk of St Paul's in a way that is reminiscent of the colonnade of St Peter's in Rome. Wren's masterpiece is a worthy successor to St Peter's, it is implied, just as London itself might lay claims to be the new Rome. The barge passing under the bridge lowering its mast, the diverse traffic passing overhead and the busy wharves that flank it east

Fig. 33 Thomas Girtin, *Detail Study for the 'Eidometropolis' Section Six: St Bride's Church, Fleet Street, from the Thames, c.* 1801, pencil on wove paper, 10.8 × 14.6 cm, Yale Center for British Art, New Haven (B1975.3.1210).

and west, however, promote the idea that this capital of a new imperial power is founded on the peaceful pursuit of trade, not martial aggression. The inclusion by Girtin at this point in his 360-degree view of an 'astonishing variety of objects', as the *Morning Herald* pointed out, 'characterise this great commercial City'.[101] The Barkers had realized this, too, but, as sections two and three of their panorama show (Fig. 25), a view taken from 25 metres to the east shifted the angle of the bridge decisively so that it is no longer linked with the cathedral in a powerful symbolic union. It is a matter of conjecture, but perhaps Girtin was influenced in his choice of view by Nathaniel Black, whose watercolour, *London, from Albion Place* (Fig. 34), was shown at the Royal Academy

in 1798.[102] It was taken from the same terrace used by Girtin, though from lower down, looking from the bow window shown in Figure 29. From here the bridge appears closer and it is populated with an even denser and more varied stream of traffic travelling to and from the City than in Girtin's view. The range and quantity of river traffic offers an even sharper contrast with the *Eidometropolis*, and Black's watercolour includes the sailing barges at the Albion Mills Wharf that Girtin pointedly omitted. The critics may have been satisfied that Girtin showed a suitable mass of human activity and busy commerce, but it was a matter of less achieving more for a more discerning audience.

Fig. 34   Nathaniel Black and Joseph Charles Barrow, *View of London, from Albion Place*, c. 1798, pencil and watercolour on wove paper, 76.5 × 132.7 cm, Museum of London (47.29).

SECTION SEVEN

The Thames from Queenhithe to London Bridge, the View Looking North East

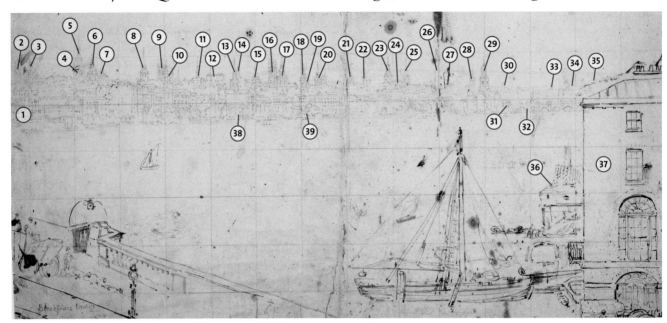

1 ST BENET PAUL'S WHARF The building was rebuilt to the designs of Robert Hooke (1678–84). It is only visible on the coloured drawing.

2 ST LAWRENCE JEWRY The church was rebuilt after the fire (1671–80) with a fine lead spire.

3 ST MARY MAGDALEN, OLD FISH STREET Rebuilt by Wren between 1683–87.

4 ALL HALLOWS, BREAD STREET A Wren church dating from 1681–84. The tower coincides with the view of:

5 ST MARY-LE-BOW, CHEAPSIDE Rebuilt by Wren in 1670–73. The tower and steeple, sixty-six metres high, is home to the famous Bow Bells.

6 ST NICHOLAS COLE ABBEY A Wren church of 1672–78, it had a hexagonal leaded spire.

7 ST OLAVE JEWRY Another church by Wren, dating from 1671–79. The tower can be seen here behind St Nicholas Cole Abbey.

8 ST MILDRED, BREAD STREET The old church was rebuilt by Wren with a dome and a lead-covered spire.

9 ST MARY ALDERMARY The Gothic building was reworked after the Great Fire with the tower rebuilt, 1701–04.

10 ST MARY SOMERSET The church was rebuilt by Wren between 1685–94. The tower, thirty-six metres high, alone remains.

11 ST ANTHOLIN, WATLING STREET Rebuilt by Wren, 1678–84.

12 THE MANSION HOUSE Designed by George Dance, the monumental structure was built between 1739–52. At this date the building was still surmounted by one of the two clerestories.

13 ST MICHAEL, QUEENHITHE The church was rebuilt by Wren in 1676–86. The distinctive steeple was built of stone and lead-covered timber.

14 ST STEPHEN WALBROOK The church was built by Wren, 1672–80.

15 ST MARY WOOLNOTH The church was rebuilt by Hawksmoor in 1716–27.

16 ST MICHAEL CORNHILL The medieval tower survived the Great Fire, but was rebuilt in 1717–22. It was possibly designed by Hawksmoor.

17 ST JAMES GARLICKHITHE The church was rebuilt by Wren between 1676–82 and the tower was finished with a steeple (1713–17) to a design possibly by Hawksmoor.

18 ST MICHAEL PATERNOSTER ROYAL The church was rebuilt by Wren from 1685–94, with a later spire, possibly after a design by Hawksmoor.

19 ST EDMUND THE KING, OR ST SWITHIN CANNON STREET The two drawings give incomplete or contradictory details here.

20 ST MARY ABCHURCH The medieval church, destroyed in the Great Fire, was rebuilt 1681–86 with a thin lead-covered spire.

21 ST BENET GRACECHURCH A Wren church with a fine tower and spire.

22 ST KATHERINE COLEMAN The church escaped destruction in the Great Fire, but was rebuilt 1739–40.

23 ST MICHAEL, CROOKED LANE The medieval church was reconstructed in 1685–88 after the Great Fire. It was pulled down in 1832 to make way for the new approach road to London Bridge.

24 ALL HALLOWS THE GREAT   Rebuilt after the Great Fire (1677–84) with a simple square tower.

25 ST MARGARET PATTENS   Wren began the rebuilding of the church in 1684 and the tower and the lead-covered spire were completed by 1702.

26 THE MONUMENT   Designed by Wren with the help of Robert Hooke, it was constructed of Portland stone in 1671–77. Its height of sixty-one metres spans the distance from where the Great Fire broke out to the east.

27 ST GEORGE, BOTOLPH LANE   Wren's church (1671–76) replaced the medieval building lost in the Great Fire.

28 ST DUNSTAN-IN-THE-EAST   The medieval church lost in the Great Fire was rebuilt, 1666–70. The later tower was designed by Wren, 1695–1701, and had a fine open-work spire.

29 ST MAGNUS THE MARTYR   The church was rebuilt by Wren, 1671–84, with a distinctive tower and cupola measuring fifty-six metres high.

30 ALL HALLOWS, BARKING, also known as ALL HALLOWS BY THE TOWER   The church has a monumental square tower dating from the 1650s.

31 LONDON BRIDGE WATERWORKS   The first three arches were occupied by waterwheels to extract water for consumers on the north bank.

32 LONDON BRIDGE   The medieval stone bridge was stripped between 1759 and 1762 of the buildings that had been added piecemeal and the central arches were replaced. Its days were numbered though. A competition was held in 1799–1801 to find a replacement, though the new five-arched structure was not built until 1823–31.

33 THE GRAND STOREHOUSE OR TOWER ARMOURY   Built in 1688–91 within the Tower walls, this large structure was burnt down in 1841.

34 THE TOWER OF LONDON   The great Norman Keep is the only part of the tower clearly visible in Girtin's view.

35 THE POOL OF LONDON   The 'forest of masts' associated with the trading heart of London at this date is barely visible.

36 ALBION MILLS WHARF

37 ALBION MILLS   This shows the domestic wing of the mill building which remained undamaged by the fire.

38 QUEENHITHE

39 THREE CRANES WHARF

The wharves and docks to the immediate east of Blackfriars Bridge create a distinctive double register of a riverbank dominated by commerce and a skyline spanned by the results of the Herculean campaign of rebuilding the City churches damaged or destroyed by the Great Fire. This horizontal division continues in the final section of Girtin's preparatory drawings, looking north east (Figs 10–11). As with the view further west (Fig. 8), the main interest is concentrated in a narrow band separated from the spectator by a substantial area of river, but the foreground intrudes into the outline drawing as it completes its 360-degree progress, terminating with the northern bay of the Albion Mills.

Contrary to many images of the fire that show the whole building engulfed in flames, Girtin correctly depicts this section as being untouched, saved by the thick party walls which separated it from the main part of the structure. The domestic accommodation that Samuel Wyatt designed for himself was therefore still in use in 1802. Closer inspection shows that the drawing does not quite complete the circle, however. The outlines for sections seven and one (Figs 10 and 1) were not cut down and there is a clear gap with one bay of Albion Mills missing. Girtin's division of the 360-degree circuit into seven sections was always likely to cause problems, but in a large

symmetrical building such as this it was relatively straightforward to fill in the missing area. All of which suggests that this was the final drawing in Girtin's sequence and that there was a *de facto* beginning and end to his circle, after all, reflecting the order in which the drawings were made.

Like the first section of the panoramic view from the Adelphi (Fig. 12), Girtin's final part of his circle (Figs 10–11) coincides with one of Canaletto's iconic London views, *The Thames on Lord Mayor's Day, Looking Towards the City and St Paul's Cathedral* (c. 1752).[103] Allowing for the way that Blackfriars Bridge intrudes into Girtin's composition, his view covers the same ground and Canaletto's prospect must therefore have been taken from very close to where Albion Place was built. But, besides the obvious emphasis on the river as a site of civic pageantry, both Canaletto's view and Black's watercolour of the north bank (Fig. 34) display a fundamental difference from Girtin's approach to topography. The even light of both Black's and Canaletto's views mean that the viewer can trace in some detail the succession of wharves and warehouses that line the bank, seeing in the former where new developments had occurred over the past fifty years. In contrast, at least half of Girtin's riverbank is cast in deep shadow; the buildings lose definition in the outline drawing (Fig. 10) and are no more than a dense mass of colour and reflections in the coloured drawing (Fig. 11). Even in the nearer stretch of the river where the sun has lit up a line of warehouses as far as the Three Cranes Wharf, it is only possible to recognize a few landmarks, such as the wharf at Queenhithe depicted in a watercolour by Charles Tomkins (Fig. 35) with the sort of clarity Girtin regularly eschewed. Instead, the artist emphasizes the different effects of sunlight and shade on the building materials, the rhythm of the repeating forms of the roofs, and, above all, the play of reflections in the river's still waters. The history and identity of the commercial buildings along this stretch of the river with their utilitarian and severely functional forms is not especially clear, but Girtin's approach here does not encourage us to look at individual buildings. The key here is Girtin's use of light which, unlike Canaletto's bright, even tone, masses structures together. The critic of *London und Paris* noted that 'the grey skies above London are artfully natural', and that

dull light effectively undermines associations between the city and its great commercial forebear, Venice.[104] Girtin's London, under its characteristically mixed English sky, does not slip into the increasingly clichéd trope of London/river, commerce/Venice that marked out much Thames imagery of the late eighteenth century.

The extraordinary succession of spires and towers that dominate this section of the London skyline are, in contrast to the riverside, much easier to identify in the two drawings, with as many as twenty-eight named on the key. The coloured drawing includes details of the materials used in the construction of many of the buildings, and this is particularly useful in confirming their identities. A number of spires and towers also appear here, but not in the outline, suggesting that the colour may have been at least partly added on the spot in this case. However, it is still not possible to identify all the buildings. Girtin, it seems, remained true to the governing principle of panoramas, that the artist takes what the view

Fig. 35   Charles Tomkins, *Queenhithe Flour Wharf*, 1801, watercolour on paper, 15 × 21 cm, London Metropolitan Archives (q7712608).

generates, confusions and occlusions alike, so that where towers align or overlap in misleading ways this is what is shown, even if it means that the identity of a building is lost. In contrast to the Barkers' later panorama in which one visitor in 1795 claimed that he had counted 'sixty-five Spires' on view, Girtin did not carefully plot a separate space for each structure.[105] Perhaps it was the same for Girtin's audience as it is for us: it was the sheer profusion of post-Fire monuments which was both the point of interest and a source of civic pride. The prominent position of the Monument, topped with its flaming urn, underlines the point.

The characteristic element of chance is again at work in the final section where the eastern part of the north bank of the Thames abruptly terminates at the roof of the first bay of the Albion Mills on the south bank (Fig. 10). The modern ruin therefore crops and occludes all but seven of the eighteen arches of Old London Bridge and leaves visible only a fragment of the Tower of London behind. From this angle we can identify the waterwheels of the London Bridge Waterworks which occupy the first three arches, but there is only the merest hint of the mass of ships in the Pool of London which commonly signified the city's status as the greatest trading centre in the world. The view from Blackfriars Bridge may include the other two London bridges then extant, but as with Westminster to the west, London Bridge and its associated historical buildings appear far from grand, if not downright mean in appearance. As the critic of *London und Paris* claimed, many of the main public buildings are 'so far away that one cannot distinguish them' and the great 'forest of masts' at the Tower appear 'the size of straws'.[106] From this point the great contemporary developments in the docks downriver of the old Legal Quays are also out of sight. The Pool of London had seen a phenomenal growth in trade and the shortage of capacity led to the building of new docks on an unprecedented scale, all of which happens offstage for a panorama from Blackfriars.[107]

Neither commercial London, the trading capital of the Empire, nor the old historic centre of the City were well represented in Girtin's final section, therefore. But, as we have seen, such topographical shortcomings were inevitable in a panorama and for the discerning visitor they would not have caused a problem. Unlike the foreign critic in search of knowledge and facts, the citizen of the capital could more easily make allowances for the view's limitations, knowing that their primary needs were experiential and that old London Bridge was worth marginalizing in favour of the dynamic thrust of the north–south axis at Blackfriars with its tripartite focus on regeneration, connection and expansion. Indeed, what made the *Eidometropolis* a 'connoisseur's panorama', in contrast to the 'common way', was as much about what could not be seen or identified in the view. Girtin's great spectacle was based on a highly detailed and topographically accurate structure, but this was disrupted by landscape effects which often inverted the hierarchy of subjects and generated a random quality, mirroring the element of chance that characterized the panorama as a new and revolutionary way of depicting the urban landscape. Sadly for the Girtin brothers, as joint entrepreneurs in the project, their attempt to give viewers something different from the common run of panoramas seems to have been interpreted as somehow lacking. The answer to the question of whether Girtin's artistic agenda was incompatible with his topographic subject takes us back to an earlier conclusion: it enhanced the status of the panorama for a limited audience of fellow 'artists', 'amateurs' and 'connoisseurs'. They were the people who could appreciate how the famed landscape watercolourist filtered the topographical subject through his imagination rather than simply enumerating the facts that fell within the 360 degrees of his view. Unfortunately for the Girtin brothers, there were just not enough 'connoisseurs' to return a profit on a project that was designed to stand out from the run-of-the-mill panoramas by pursuing a fine art agenda.

A guide to sites visible from Girtin's viewpoint on the roof of Albion Place

Section 1 – The Albion Mills, the View Looking South East

The view is dominated by the façade of the Albion Mills. The most significant landmarks are listed on the key on page 46.

Section 2 – Great Surrey Street and Christ Church, Southwark, the View Looking South

The majority of the buildings identified on the key on page 49 were constructed after the completion of Blackfriars Bridge in 1769.

Section 3 – Lambeth and Westminster, the View Looking South West

The key on page 51 lists the historical sites in the distance and the more humble housing in the foreground.

Section 4 - The Thames from Westminster to Somerset House, the View Looking West

The industrial sites in the foreground and the buildings seen on the north bank of the river are listed on the key on page 54.

Section 5 - The Thames from the Temple to Blackfriars, the View Looking North West

The buildings on the north bank of the Thames are listed on the key on page 57.

Section 6 - Blackfriars Bridge and St Paul's Cathedral, the View Looking North

The section is dominated by the massive form of St Paul's. Many of the other buildings erected after the Great Fire are listed on the key on page 59.

Section 7 - The Thames from Queenhithe to London Bridge, the View Looking North East

The key on page 62 identifies 28 of the towers and spires which dominate the skyline as the view joins the Albion Mills south of the river.

Fig. 36 Detail from Richard Horwood's *Map of London* (1799) marked with some of the sites depicted in Girtin's *Eidometropolis*.

POSTSCRIPT
A new fate for Girtin's London panorama

The viewpoint Girtin used for his panorama, Albion Place Terrace, has long since been demolished; indeed, the replacement of its replacement is set to open this year. *One Blackfriars* will top out at fifty storeys and any artist prepared to try to take a panoramic view from the top would look down distantly on a city that continues to transform itself at a dizzying speed and would be unrecognizable, except in a few areas, to an original spectator of the *Eidometropolis*. The *Morning Herald* in its obituary of Girtin was concerned by the fate of his panorama after it ended its commercial showing, suggesting that it might be 'fitted up, and form an elegant object in a Nobleman or Gentleman's park' so that 'the Antiquary in a few years would see what London was, and mark the great alterations that are about to take place'.[108] Thomas Girtin's widow, who took over the running of the panorama after the artist's death, took a different view, running an advertisement that stated that the 'Picture is to be disposed of, and is well worthy the attention of any Gentleman going abroad, as it was painted by the late Mr. GIRTIN for that purpose'.[109] And, following the suggestion of Stephan Oettermann, it has been generally accepted that the *Eidometropolis* was returned to Paris where it was displayed in 1804–05 and 1806 before perishing in a fire in Lyons in 1807.[110] Reviews in *London und Paris* specifically state that this London view, unlike the Barkers' panorama which was also shown in Paris in 1802, was taken from the 'glasshouses near Blackfriar's Bridge' or 'as if from the glass manufactory on the edge of the city at Blackfriars Bridge'.[111] Both of the locations are, as we have seen, incorrect and it has been assumed that the new proprietor followed the erroneous description of the Girtin brothers without any reason, or the means, to check its accuracy.

A new possibility has, however, recently emerged which, whilst it does not necessarily contradict the idea that the *Eidometropolis* was shown in Paris, suggests that it may also have toured Eastern Europe two decades later. The recent online publication of Ralph Hyde's unfinished *Dictionary of Panoramists* includes a reference to the discovery by the panorama specialist, Gabriele Koller, of a London panorama which appeared in St Petersburg in 1821 under the aegis of Johann Friedrich Tielker (1768–1832), and then toured to Riga, Königsberg, Berlin, Vienna, Leipzig, Dresden and, finally, to Munich in 1828.[112] Koller has also identified a key to the panorama and this shows that it was taken from Girtin's viewpoint, with all of the buildings visible in the 360-degree circle occupying the same relative positions.[113] One of the reviews identified by Koller also mentions a group of 'brutish boxers' near Blackfriars Bridge, which, as we have seen, featured in Girtin's panorama, though not in the studies for that section (Figs 1–2).[114] The plan, it must be admitted, also contains features not present in Girtin's *Eidometropolis*, including Southwark Bridge, opened in 1819 and Waterloo Bridge which preceded it in 1817. But, as Ralph Hyde argued, these could have been added to an older canvas, a practice that was common at this time, and this panorama, as a contemporary reviewer noted, was worn out from travelling and had been painted some twenty years earlier. There are outstanding questions still to be determined, but Koller's invaluable research opens up the real possibility that the *Eidometropolis* ended up in Russia, as Girtin family tradition had it all along.[115]

NOTES

1 Hubert J. Pragnell, *The London Panoramas of Robert Barker and Thomas Girtin*, London Topographical Society No. 109 (London, 1968).

2 London, The National Archives, Prob. 6/179, f. 616. The document is published in full in Greg Smith, 'Girtin v Girtin: New information on a panorama of London by Thomas Girtin (1775–1802) and his *Picturesque Views in Paris*', *The British Art Journal*, 18, no. 3 (Winter 2017/18), 28–47. This supplements, and in some cases corrects, the earlier account in Greg Smith, *Thomas Girtin: The Art of Watercolour*, exhibition catalogue, London, Tate Britain (London, 2002), pp. 189–205.

3 Ralph Hyde and Peter Jackson, *London from the Roof of the Albion Mills: A Facsimile of Robert and Henry Aston Barker's Panorama of 1792–3*, London Topographical Society No. 139, published in association with the Guildhall Library (London, 1988).

4 Paul Laxton, 'Richard Horwood's Map and the Face of London, 1799–1819', in *The A to Z of Regency London*, London Topographical Society No. 131, published in association with the Guildhall Library and Harry Margary (Lympne Castle, Kent, 1985).

5 The drawings were with the Fine Art Society, London, in 1912 and it appears that they were sold at Christie's, 1 April 1911, as lot 124 'Panorama of London' by 'Turner and Girtin', though the measurements do not match those for the missing drawings seen in the old photographs. Another panoramic scene listed as 'Drawing: A long panoramic view of the Thames (Surrey side) from Blackfriars to Westminster' in sepia, was sold at Sotheby's later in the year (8 December, lot 171) with very different, presumably erroneous, measurements ('16½ × 5 ft. 7ins').

6 Girtin and Loshak in their catalogue of Girtin's work reproduce only the first section from Somerset House to the Shot Tower, missing the full extent of the river view (Thomas Girtin and David Loshak, *The Art of Thomas Girtin* (London, 1954), pp. 58–59, fig. 24).

7 For the work that the two artists produced for Monro, see Smith, *Thomas Girtin*, pp. 123–27.

8 Christie's, 28 June 1833, lot 50. The drawings were sold to Monro's son, Alexander, and they may have remained in the family throughout the rest of the century.

9 For a concise and well-illustrated account of the characteristic panoramic Thames views, west and east, influenced by Canaletto, see Michael Liversidge and Jane Farington (eds), *Canaletto & England*, exhibition catalogue, Birmingham Museums and Art Gallery (London, 1993). Girtin copied prints after Canaletto, and Monro owned a number of the Venetian master's drawings. See Smith, *Thomas Girtin*, p. 130, and Girtin and Loshak, *The Art of Thomas Girtin*, nos 221–24.

10 The drawing is in the collection of the Courtauld Institute Galleries (D.1978.PG.131), but it would have been known to artists from the engraving by Edward Rooker.

11 The matching view (London, British Museum (G,13.31)) measures 53 × 191.6 cm.

12 Erik Hinterding, Ger Luijten and Martin Royalton-Kisch, *Rembrandt the Printmaker*, exhibition catalogue, London, British Museum, and Amsterdam, Rijksmuseum (London, 2000), pp. 184–86. The text describes how *Landscape with a Cottage and Large Tree* and *Landscape with a Cottage and Haybarn* make up a continuous extended view flanking the central etching of Amsterdam.

13 London, British Museum (1880, 1113.1323).

14 It was inscribed by Frederick Crace, part of whose collection of London topographical material passed to the British Museum (and was catalogued online with the help of a grant from the London Topographical Society). Malton's sale was held at Christie's, 4 May 1804, and this was lot 65. The drawing may have been purchased by the publisher William Richardson who subsequently commissioned the etching.

15 Thomas Malton, *A Picturesque Tour Through the Cities of London and Westminster*, 2 vols (London, 1792–1801), I, 59–60.

16 The drawing was until recently attributed to J. M. W. Turner.

17 *View of London* (London, British Museum (1880, 0911.564)) is dated 1803.

18 Titled *London from the Thames, S. W. of Blackfriars Bridge*, it was included in James Storer and John Greig, *Select Views of London and its Environs*, 2 vols (London, 1804–05).

19 Other watercolours showing similar views of the industrial south bank with Blackfriars Bridge and St Paul's to the left are in the collections of the National Gallery of Scotland, Edinburgh (D.4832) and the Ashmolean Museum, Oxford (Brown 752).

20 A later inscription on the verso reads 'part of scheme for his Panorama of the Thames banks'.

21 For one such scene, see Smith, *Thomas Girtin*, no. 178.

22 Two of Girtin's prints for his *Picturesque Views in Paris*, including a panoramic *General View of Paris, Taken from Chaillot*, were painted as drop curtains for Charles Dibdin's pantomime, *Wizard's Wake; or Harlequin's Regeneration* (1802).

23 *The Morning Post*, 2 August 1802, p. 1.

24 Girtin and Loshak, *The Art of Thomas Girtin*, pp. 34–35.

25 *The Morning Chronicle*, 14 October 1801, p. 1.

26 Smith, 'Girtin v Girtin', pp. 41–42.

27 The patent held by Robert Barker expired in May 1801 and this may have prompted Girtin's interest in producing a panorama.

28 Smith, 'Girtin v Girtin', p. 29.

29 *The Morning Post*, 1 February 1802, p. 2.

30 Stephan Oettermann, *The Panorama: History of a Mass Medium* (New York, 1997), pp. 147–49.

31   Smith, 'Girtin v Girtin', p. 30.

32   Edward Edwards, *Anecdotes of Painters* (London, 1808), p. 280.

33   *The Morning Chronicle*, 14 October 1801, p. 1.

34   Ralph Hyde, *Dictionary of Panoramists of the English-Speaking World*, p. 20 <http://www.bdcmuseum.org.uk/uploads/uploads/biographical_dictionary_of_panoramists2.pdf> [accessed on 17 December 2017].

35   *London und Paris*, 19 (1807), 331.

36   *The Monthly Magazine*, 14, part 2 (October 1802), 255.

37   The posthumous sale of John Girtin's father-in-law John Jackson contained '342 – Two unfinished Views of London, Blackfriar's Bridge, &c.' and '345 – Two ditto, Blackfriars Bridge, &c.' (Foster's, 22 April 1828).

38   *The Monthly Magazine*, 14, part 2 (October 1802), 255.

39   *Bell's Weekly Messenger*, 24 October 1802, p. 4.

40   In addition to numerous newspaper reports, the rivalry is detailed in two early histories of pugilism, both published anonymously: [Pierce Egan], *Boxiana; or, Sketches of Antient & Modern Pugilism* (London, 1812) and *Pancratia, or a History of Pugilism* (London, 1812). I would like to acknowledge the help of Tony Gee, the Prize-Fighter Historian, who checked this section of my text.

41   Craig's illustrations were published as an addendum to Richard Phillips, *Modern London; Being the History and Present State of the British Metropolis* (London, 1804). The end of the bridge is also the territory of *The Old Ballad Singer, John Massey*, in a mezzotint of 1775 by John Raphael Smith after George Carter (London, British Museum (1902, 1011.5007)).

42   John Girtin noted that he paid £38 11s. 6d. 'for advertisements in the different newspapers' (Smith, 'Girtin v Girtin', p. 43).

43   *The Morning Post*, 2 August 1802, p. 1.

44   *The Times*, 25 August 1802, p. 1.

45   *The Morning Chronicle*, 18 August 1802, p. 1.

46   *The Morning Post*, 8 September 1802, p. 1.

47   Hyde and Jackson, *London from the Roof of the Albion Mills*, n.p.

48   *The Observer*, 8 August 1802, p. 3. Ironically, the only time the Girtins identified the building as a 'Warehouse' was in the very first advertisement (*The Morning Post*, 2 August 1802, p. 1).

49   *The Times*, 22 September 1802, p. 1.

50   *The Morning Post*, 22 October 1802, p. 1.

51   *Bell's Weekly Messenger*, 31 October 1802, p. 7.

52   *The Morning Post*, 23 November 1802, p. 1; *The Morning Chronicle*, 3 March 1803, p. 1. All of the advertisements quoted here were repeated, some with minor variations, and more no doubt wait to be discovered.

53   This is taken from the *Prospectus* John produced for Thomas Girtin's posthumously published *Picturesque Views in Paris*. The only known surviving copy is in the library of the Sir John Soane's Museum, London (ref. no. 2347).

54   *The Monthly Magazine*, 14, part 2 (October 1802), 255; *The Morning Herald*, 6 December 1802.

55   Ibid.

56   *The Morning Herald*, 19 November 1802.

57   *The Observer*, 8 August 1802, p. 3.

58   *Bell's Weekly Messenger*, 15 August 1802, p. 6.

59   *The Monthly Magazine*, 14, part 2 (October 1802), 254.

60   The costs and the income generated by the *Eidometropolis* are discussed in more detail in Smith, 'Girtin v Girtin', pp. 30–32.

61   Denise Blake Oleksijczuk, *The First Panoramas: Visions of British Imperialism* (Minnesota, 2011), p. 6.

62   Advertisements found in the following newspapers establish the scale of the tour, as well as giving valuable information on the panorama itself: *Hull Advertiser and Exchange Gazette*, 1 September 1798; *Newcastle Courant*, 19 October 1799; *Caledonian Mercury, Edinburgh*, 15 March 1800; *Aberdeen Press and Journal*, 6 April 1801; *Glasgow Courier*, 1 July 1801; *Manchester Mercury*, 2 February 1802; *Bath Chronicle and Weekly Gazette*, 13 January 1803; *Oxford Journal*, 23 April 1803; *Saunders's News Letter, Dublin*, 6 August 1803.

63   *Aberdeen Press and Journal*, 6 April 1801.

64   Cooper's career is unravelled in the excellent website dedicated to the Scottish artist Hugh William Williams, edited by Joe Rock (https://sites.google.com/site/hughwilliamwilliams/). The Edinburgh showing of the *Grand Perspective Panorama* is noted by Scott Wilcox in his dissertation ('The Panorama and Related Exhibitions in London', MLitt dissertation, University of Edinburgh, 1976, pp. 226–27), and I would like to take this opportunity to thank Scott for his generous help and support with this project.

65   Barker's drawings, made in May 1802, are in the collection of the Victoria and Albert Museum, London (D.1456/63-1903).

66   *The Monthly Magazine*, 14, part 2 (October 1802), 255.

67   The architecture of the Albion Mills, as well as its significance in the history of engineering, are well covered in A. W. Skempton, 'Samuel Wyatt and the Albion Mill', *Architectural History*, 14 (1971), 53–73, and John Mosse, 'The Albion Mills, 1784–1791', *The Newcomen Society Transactions*, 40 (1967–68), 47–60.

68   See 'Conflagration! The Burning of the Albion Mill, Southwark, in 1791', in B. E. Maidment, *Reading Popular Prints 1790–1870* (Manchester and New York, 1996), p. 27.

69   Ibid., p. 37.

70   Kenneth G. Farries and Martin T. Mason, *The Windmills of Surrey and Inner London* (London, 1966), p. 204, fig. 106.

71   [George Griffin Stonestreet], *Domestic Union, or London as it Should Be!!* (London, 1800), p. 6.

72   *The Monthly Magazine*, 14, part 2 (October 1802), 255.

73   For examples of the bird's-eye view and its capacity for showing the full extent of the modern city at this date, see Ralph Hyde, *Gilded Scenes and Shining Prospects: Panoramic Views of British Towns, 1575–1900*, exhibition catalogue, New Haven, Yale Center for British Art (New Haven, 1985), pp. 150–65.

74   See Bernard Nurse, *London: Prints & Drawings Before 1800*, London Topographical Society No. 179 (Oxford and London, 2017).

75   *The Morning Herald*, 6 December 1802.

76   *Bell's Weekly Messenger*, 15 August 1802, p. 6.

77   The church, which no longer exists, is the subject of an earlier pencil drawing by Girtin (New Haven, Yale Center for British Art, B1975.3.1156).

78   *London und Paris*, 14 (1804), 52.

79   *The Monthly Magazine*, 14, part 2 (October 1802), 255.

80   Ann Bermingham, 'Landscape-O-Rama: The Exhibition Landscape at Somerset House and the Rise of Popular Landscape Entertainments', in *Art on the Line: The Royal Academy Exhibitions at Somerset House 1780–1836*, ed. by David H. Solkin (New Haven and London, 2001), p. 136.

81   It has not been possible to identify the low horseshoe-shaped building in front of that.

82 The most useful introduction to the expansion of London at this date and the role of speculative building is Andrew Saint, 'The Building Art of the First Industrial Metropolis', in *London — World City: 1800–1840*, ed. by Celina Fox, exhibition catalogue, Essen, Villa Hügel (New Haven and London, 1992), pp. 51–76.

83 See Farries and Mason, *Windmills*, pp. 132–33 for the Lambeth mills. The Sandby watercolour is in the collection of the British Museum, London (1978, 0520.8).

84 *London und Paris*, 14 (1804), 52; 19 (1807), 332.

85 *The Monthly Magazine*, 14, part 2 (October 1802), 255.

86 *The Morning Post*, 22 October 1802, p. 1.

87 *The Morning Herald*, 6 December 1802.

88 *The Monthly Magazine*, 14, part 2 (October 1802), 255.

89 Anonymous, *The Thames, London, the Surrey Bank with Lukin's Iron Foundry and the Shot Tower, c. 1800* (Manchester, Whitworth Art Gallery, D.1926.100).

90 The Patent Shot Tower, 42 metres high, was built in 1789 for the inventor of the process, William Watt. Molten lead was dropped from a height to form perfectly spherical shot under the influence of gravity.

91 James Peller Malcolm, *Londinium Redivivum; or, an Ancient History and Modern Description of London*, 2 vols (London, 1802), I, 11–12.

92 John Brewer, 'Sensibility and the Urban Panorama', *Huntington Library Quarterly*, 70, no. 2 (June 2007), 237.

93 *The Monthly Magazine*, 14, part 2 (October 1802), 255.

94 The New River Company, founded in the early seventeenth century to bring fresh water from Hertfordshire to the capital, had grown to great prosperity, commissioning a smart classical building from Colen Campbell as its offices.

95 *The Morning Herald*, 6 December 1802.

96 The view of St Bride's has only recently been associated with the panorama. Because of its utilitarian and rather prosaic appearance it was previously dated to *c.* 1792.

97 See note 37. For the early provenances of Girtin's two sets of preparatory drawings, see Smith, 'Girtin v Girtin', p. 38.

98 *The Monthly Magazine*, 14, part 2 (October 1802), 255.

99 William Combe, *A History of the River Thames*, 2 vols (London, 1796), I, 213.

100 *The Morning Herald*, 6 December 1802.

101 Ibid.

102 The view was engraved by Joseph Stadler and published in May 1802 (London Metropolitan Archives, q897256x).

103 The work, now in the Lobkowicz Collection at Prague Castle, has only recently been seen again in this country having been sent to Bohemia in 1752. See Susan Doran and Robert J. Blyth, eds, *Royal River: Power, Pageantry and the Thames*, exhibition catalogue, Greenwich, National Maritime Museum (London, 2012).

104 *London und Paris*, 19 (1807), 332.

105 William MacRitchie, *Diary of a Tour Through Great Britain in 1795* (London, 1897), p. 83.

106 *London und Paris*, 19 (1807), 331. See Geoffrey William Snell, 'A Forest of Masts: The Image of the River in the Long Eighteenth Century' (doctoral thesis, University of Sussex, 2014).

107 See Saint, 'Building Art', pp. 51–54.

108 *The Morning Herald*, 6 December 1802.

109 *Bell's Weekly Messenger*, 9 January 1803, p. 14.

110 Oettermann, *Panorama*, p. 149. This was certainly my view in 2002 (Smith, *Thomas Girtin*, p. 193).

111 *London und Paris*, 19 (1807), 331; 14 (1804), 52.

112 Hyde, *Panoramists*, pp. 188–89.

113 Gabriele Koller has very generously shared her research on Tielker with me, together with an image of the key. This material will feature in her forthcoming doctoral thesis, 'The Panorama in the Context of Art Exhibitions, Late Eighteenth to Mid-Nineteenth Century', and hopefully also in a substantial publication of the fascinating story she has uncovered.

114 *Rigaische Stadt-Blatter fur das Jahr 1821* (Riga, 1822), pp. 265–67.

115 See Girtin and Loshak, *Thomas Girtin*, p. 36 for the origins of the story.

INDEX